Corporate Brand Personality

Re-focus your organization's culture to build trust, respect and authenticity

Lesley Everett

KoganPage

LONDON PHILADELPHIA NEW DELHI

First published in Great Britain and the United States in 2016 by Kogan Page Limited

2nd Floor, 45 Gee Street
London
EC1V 3RS
United Kingdom

1518 Walnut Street, Suite 1100
Philadelphia PA 19102
USA

4737/23 Ansari Road
Daryaganj
New Delhi 110002
India

© Lesley Everett, 2016

The right of Lesley Everett to be identified as the author of this work has been asserted by her in accordance with the Copyright, Designs and Patents Act 1988.

ISBN   978 0 7494 7137 8
E-ISBN   978 0 7494 7138 5

British Library Cataloguing-in-Publication Data

A CIP record for this book is available from the British Library.   659.285

Library of Congress Cataloging-in-Publication Data

Names: Everett, Lesley, author.
Title: Corporate brand personality : re-focus your organization's culture to
    build trust, respect and authenticity / Lesley Everett.
Description: philadelphia : Kogan Page, 2016.
Identifiers: LCCN 2015040425 | ISBN 9780749471378 (paperback)
Subjects: LCSH: Branding (Marketing) | Social responsibility of business. |
    Corporate culture. | Consumer behavior. | BISAC: BUSINESS & ECONOMICS /
    Strategic Planning. | BUSINESS & ECONOMICS / Leadership. | BUSINESS &
    ECONOMICS / Management.
Classification: LCC HF5415.1255 .E93 2016 | DDC 658.8/27–dc23 LC record available at
http://lccn.loc.gov/2015040425

Typeset by Graphicraft Limited, Hong Kong
Print production managed by Jellyfish
Printed and bound by CPI Group (UK) Ltd, Croydon CR0 4YY

*To two amazing men who I am so grateful to
every day for being in my life:*

Chris Swainson – my man, my bear, my rock

*Max Everett – my awesome, Gen Y son.
I'm so proud of you*

CONTENTS

07   Presentational brand   165

08   Final words   187

FOREWORD
By Sir Clive Woodward

A great team is made up of great individuals.

This book provides your business, whatever the size, with the necessary components to powerfully maximize your corporate brand investment via your people and team behaviours.

My own career has covered both business and sport. I spent 16 years in business: eight years working for Rank Xerox in the United Kingdom and Australia and eight years running my own small leasing company. I then went on to become the first full-time professional coach of the England rugby team, leading them to World Cup success in 2003 and Director of Sport for Team GB for the London Olympics 2012.

From my years in business and in sport I have learnt one key thing: 'In order to get things right on the field of play you must get things right off the field of play.'

I have learnt, and subsequently speak about, the importance that each individual in a team plays in this concept. Without each individual's adherence, input and belief in the Team objective, success becomes more of a game of chance than of certainty.

The real importance of every individual taking personal responsibility for their actions and behaviours is absolutely fundamental to creating a successful business team. This is what Lesley articulates so well in this excellent book.

Lesley expertly provides the know-how and tools you need in order for your people to consistently represent the brand of your organization. She shares her insights from her years of experience on the topic of personal branding and the knowledge gathered as a result of practical global corporate engagements, media discussions, interviews and articles.

This highly informed account is the culmination of this extensive work and it demonstrates that how we conduct ourselves in business has a huge effect on our bottom line – and can have an even more profound impact on it than the vast array of other complex commercial decisions facing businesses.

We buy from people, not companies. This is a fact that runs through this book from beginning to end.

There is nobody better to write a book on this subject than Lesley Everett. Her experience over many years of researching, specializing, designing training programmes and speaking globally, position her as *the* expert in this field.

I have personally experienced Lesley's world-class work and expertise in this critical area of business. I have also witnessed her present her powerful message to large corporate audiences with the compelling impact that the subject matter deserves.

The perfect timing for this book is right now. Every business owner, every leader in an organization, and every coach should read it, absorb it and follow Lesley's advice.

Your customers will decide your brand for you based on their experience with your people. You simply cannot ignore the fact that today your people come first when it comes to your brand.

FOREWORD
by Andy Clarke, President and CEO of Asda Walmart

Serving 18 million customers, our Asda colleagues represent our brand every day. Watch our advertising and you'll see real colleagues front and centre of every campaign. Talk to anyone in the retail industry and they'll tell you that what makes Asda special is the personality of its colleagues.

That doesn't happen by accident. It's a vital part of Asda's unique culture which connects everyone, from the shop floor to the boardroom. Understanding and developing our culture is key to our success, and we regularly invest in its health. That includes working alongside Lesley Everett, who has supported me and my leadership team for a number of years.

Lesley's Brand Me programme helped us revitalize our culture at a challenging time for the industry, and she played a key role in establishing our award-winning Women in Leadership programme.

Many of the lessons and techniques that Lesley embedded into Asda are explored in this book, and that's why I'm recommending it to business leaders. Our continuing relationship with Lesley keeps me and my leadership team focused on the culture of our business, and that's what drives our bottom line.

PREFACE

The creation of this book has been a thoroughly rewarding experience and I'm excited to hear your views.

I feel the time is right for this subject to be brought to the attention of business owners and senior directors in this way. There is finally an appetite to not just acknowledge the massive impact that people behaviours have on our corporate brand and reputation today, but to actually want to know how to take control and implement strategies to manage it.

For the past five years I have focused particularly on the risk to businesses in not investing in this area and have presented the topic to and worked with thousands of executives around the globe. I finally feel we have some traction and it is starting to gain the wider attention it deserves.

The content in this book is not based on academia but rather on real experience or interactive research as I call it, with many global businesses. I have witnessed some of the most sophisticated approaches to branding and to learning and development; but rarely have I come across a business that puts the necessary level of investment into the areas that make the real competitive difference in a commercial world that demands trust and relies on positive relationships to be successful.

I hope that my book will inspire you to analyse your business more deeply in this respect and encourage you to build techniques and strategies to effectively manage brand personality. Ultimately, I want to see you being talked about in the media and across social media in a way that truly builds a level of trust, respect and authenticity that you and your clients have never witnessed before.

Thank you for reading and especially for your interest in enhancing the levels of authenticity in our business world today.

ACKNOWLEDGEMENTS

There are some very important people I would like to thank who helped make this book possible.

Firstly my parents, who continue to give me the best possible reason to feel proud of my achievements, no matter how small. Thanks, Mum and Dad, for all your love and support.

Prof Dr Bernd Ankenbrand, who provided invaluable academic viewpoint, research and sanity checks in the early days of the book's creation.

Vicky Whitehouse for your incredible attention to detail and grammatical correction. Victoria Donahue and Judy Jones for providing your broader perspective.

Alan Stevens and Sean Weafer, my Mastermind buddies, for your input and support. Andy Lopata, Sam Silverstein, Mike Kerr, Dr Graeme Codrington, Shaun Smith, Doug Stevenson for your valuable contributions.

My clients and colleagues who provided their time, expertise and experience for the numerous interviews.

I cannot end without thanking Bookworks Coffee Shop and Bookstore in Pacific Grove, California, where the book really materialized. A special mention for Toni and all the staff there who made me endless double mochas!

Lastly yet most importantly Chris and Max, who have tirelessly put up with and listened to my frustrations, provided reviews and given valuable perspective where needed. Chris, I know how pleased you are that this book is completed! I'm back in the business now and pleased to 'be back' as your wife.

Introduction

A misalignment of brand expectations

You walk into the reception area of a large management consultancy firm you are hoping to partner with. The decor is refreshing, sophisticated and high quality with fresh flowers, glossy brochures and an open, welcoming reception desk. Just as you would expect from their branding and advertising. Clearly this company has invested heavily in its office furnishings, the impression it wants to give to clients and its overall brand image.

Behind the reception desk are two receptionists having a chat, seemingly indifferent to the fact you are there. After a few seconds too long, you are met with an unsmiling face from one of them, indifferent in her approach, wearing clothes that are inappropriate to the professional environment. It feels like you are an inconvenience to her as she eventually looks up at you. And then, 'Yes, can I help you?' Even though she has seen you only last week, she shows no sign of recognition.

Which is the stronger, more powerful and memorable message of the consultancy firm brand? Which one do you take away with you, perhaps subconsciously, and potentially talk about with colleagues and friends? On the other hand, which is the one most heavily invested in? I would guess that the most memorable one is the attitude and behaviour of the receptionist. Why? Because it's more personal and seemingly directed at you. You feel insignificant, unimportant, undervalued, and it therefore has an emotional impact on you that sticks. These emotions are guaranteed to cause us to feel negative energy. I would also suggest that there has been more investment in the office surroundings than in the training of the receptionists. Overall your experience of the brand is likely to be largely negative.

This is a simple, non-sophisticated example; however, trust and respect in your corporate brand today does not come just from your logos, advertising and sponsorship. It comes from the people within your organization and how they communicate in all forms, to all stakeholders. That is quite simply your strongest brand messaging today and in the eyes of your customers and stakeholders, your people *are* your brand. Yes, of course you need the

FIGURE 0.1   The corporate brand reality

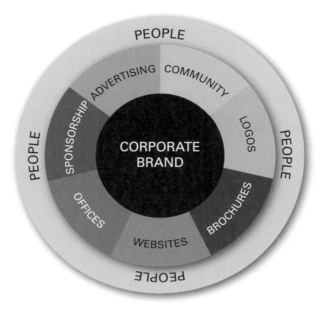

heavy investment in your websites, advertising and all your marketing collateral, which serves to create the expectation and lays out the value and guarantee of quality in the brand. The true brand value though is in the experience your clients and customers take away with them and ultimately remember and talk about.

This book will follow the roadmap below, taking you from where you may be now in the corporate world, to where you need to get to with regard to real elements of corporate branding. Running a small consultancy and training business that focuses totally on, and specializes in, the people element of the corporate brand, my team and I have had the privilege of working with many global organizations in most sectors, across 25 countries and five continents, and many different cultures. As such, I have attempted to provide you with real-life experiences you can relate to, challenges that our clients have been up against for you to familiarize yourself with, and solutions for you to refer to so that you can address the needs of your own business. While I do not focus on how you create your corporate imaging and logos, nor the entire customer experience programme that some specialist brand agencies will provide, I will help you to maximize your investment to a level that you may not have achieved before. This book will help you to align people behaviours with your brand, enhance the personality of

FIGURE 0.2   The real corporate brand journey

Destination = Maximized Corporate Brand Investment

the brand and sustain this to a level that creates positive authentic impact every time any stakeholder interacts with or experiences your organization.

The destination = maximized corporate brand investment and positive customer experience.

Most valuable brand asset

The most valuable element of your brand today is what your customers say about your brand to their contacts. In this age of digital communications, this instantly goes global through the medium of TripAdvisor, Yelp and a myriad of social media sites. With Generation Y (often referred to as the 'Millennials') and Generation Z (those that follow on from Generation Y), largely reliant on and influenced by social media and technology for their choices on where to go to bank, eat, drink, exercise and a wealth of other activities, this need is not going to disappear. If you're serious about your brand – which you will be of course – you cannot afford not to invest in aligning people behaviour with your brand messages.

Every year millions of dollars are invested by organizations in branding and re-branding, to get that logo or latest slogan at the hottest sports venues or on that prime spot billboard. How much of that investment are you wasting by not aligning people brand and behaviours to the corporate messaging and in engaging all your people in what the messaging really means? Brand-awareness building is all great and worthwhile if it is backed up consistently from all angles, and most of that means via your people. If you leave this to chance, then the leakage of brand investment could be massive.

Going even further, I would ask if you've considered the actual *risk* to your business in *not* addressing this potential leakage and dilution seriously. What if your fabulous new and expensive marketing campaign has attracted great media coverage, positive social media discussion and huge brand awareness, yet the customer experience starts to fall short of the high expectations you have created? There is an even greater height to fall from that may cost millions of dollars in lost loyalty, trust and a feeling of being 'let down'. It's fair to say that companies today don't necessarily need to exceed customer expectations as often as is thought and strived for; they just need to meet expectations consistently. It is this consistency that is lacking for the majority.

So going back to the receptionist scenario, would you consider this experience a 'hiccup' or would it have seriously tainted your view of the corporate brand? I suspect this will very much depend on previous experiences and how much of a reputation they already have with you. If this were a first experience on the other hand, your sub-conscious or even conscious brain will tell you that that is simply the way they do business, with an indifferent approach to people behaviour and customer experience; therefore, you will quite possibly question having any business dealings with them.

The brand roadblock

We are at a point in our business environment, where we need to re-align the corporate culture with that demanded by our clients and customers. Today customers demand trust, respect and a level of 'personality' from the companies they choose to buy from and build relationships with. Conversely, however, what is happening is a slide towards the other extreme, of corporate bad manners and apathy in the way businesses communicate with their stakeholders. Communication turnaround and response times are getting

FIGURE 0.3   The brand roadblock

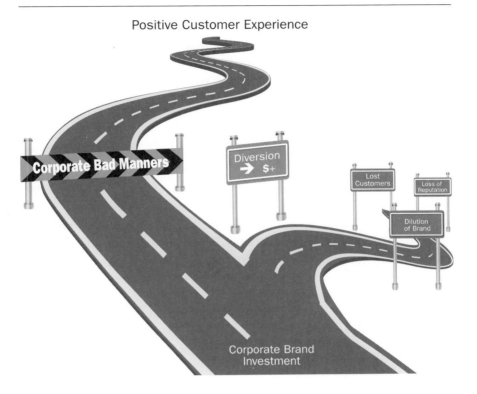

longer, and call waiting times extended in the ever-burgeoning call centre systems we all so frequently have to endure. In turn, this can create a significant roadblock between your customers and your brand, and the business success you strive for, need and work hard to achieve.

The roadblock is unfortunately becoming more firmly rooted in business culture, creating a superficial yet very effective and solid barrier to providing great customer experience and therefore ultimately increased or even static bottom-line profits. The more firmly it takes hold, and the longer it is there, the more difficult it is to change the perception of the brand, both internally and externally, as well as the resulting culture within the organization. The roadblock also creates the need for a diversion, as customers and clients try to find an easier and less troublesome and a more pleasurable way to get what they need. The unfortunate result will be a diversion away from your brand, towards other suppliers and partners.

Consider call centres as an example – was this decentralization trend a false economy? The idea of transferring call handling for customers to cheaper set-ups in other parts of the world seemed a good one for streamlining a business, taking away something that could quite easily be outsourced and in a potentially more cost-effective way. However, as has now been proven, customers want person-to-person contact more than anything, in order to 'trust' a company and its products and services. Remove that personal contact and you remove what is essentially at the core of customer loyalty, trust and respect. We are, therefore, starting to see some organizations bring call handling and customer service back in-house.

The First Direct model

Did First Direct bank in fact get it right, a long time before their competitors even saw the need for this level of localization and personalization and its resulting genius? First Direct are one of the world's first fully functional direct banks, having launched in 1989. They pioneered the concept of no branches and a 24-hour service via a call centre. In the early 1990s this model expanded to include internet banking and other banks came on-board with the concept.

When speaking with First Direct clients, I found that from the start First Direct have been consistent with their approach in really putting the customer first, and not just claiming to – they have always delivered on what they promised from the outset.

They have created a relationship with their customers that causes individuals to feel like they belong, that they can relate to their bank in a personal way and are actually valued as a customer. It is an informal brand that is human, friendly, fun and can be identified with – similar to Apple and the relationship they have created with customers. The Apple approach is totally focused on the customer from the moment they enter the store, to understanding their individual and specific needs, listening actively and providing a solution. However, this level of service and customer focus is quite incredible for a bank that has no branches!

Their call centres have no automated phone system – but instead a positive, upbeat and real person to speak to. A certain way to attract new customers and keep their existing ones happy! Again this is the personal approach that appears to be so unusual today. When calling my dentist, even when they answer my call and ask me if I mind holding, I'm quite happy to do this for two or three minutes and possibly longer if necessary, because I've had some human contact. Whereas being put in a queue for an indefinite period without that real person speaking to me, I'm unlikely to hold, even though they keep telling me my call is important to them!

From my research, I have also found a common theme to be that First Direct customers are loyal – most I spoke to have been customers for 10 or more years – and they have consistently recommended the bank over the years and actively seek out opportunities to jump in and recommend, whether in an online discussion or among colleagues. Imagine how many new customers have resulted from this. When we have a recommendation from a trusted friend or colleague, we are much more likely to try that new service. If we hear it recommended several times over from different sources, the chances of us trying it are significantly increased. Hence my belief that the most valuable part of any organization's brand today is what your customers *say* about your brand to their contacts.

> Your corporate brand today is what your customers say about your brand to their contacts

On their website, First Direct say they are 'currently the most recommended bank'. I think this is because the loyalty goes two ways – they have customer loyalty because they are also loyal to their customers with this consistent, personal and high level of service. They operate on the basis that 'people buy people'. This is what many organizations say they do; but in reality they miss the mark.

The power of positive customer experience

Research by Forrester (Burns, 2012) shows us that there is a direct correlation between customer experience and increased revenue. The research showed a high correlation between consumers' rating of a firm in the Customer Experience Index (CXi) and their willingness to buy from the company again. In addition, it significantly affected their likelihood of recommending that company, and the higher the score the less likely that customer is to go elsewhere.

In simple terms, better customer experience can drive millions of dollars in revenue benefit. The Forrester Research demonstrates that companies that move from below average to above average in the CXi are likely to have more customers who are willing to buy from them again. They found that if only a fraction of customers make another purchase in the same year, the effect on revenue can range from $15 million for retailers, to as much as $788 million for wireless service providers. Hotels and airlines also rank highly in terms of benefit from above average CXi. It may appear to be more relevant to the hospitality sectors perhaps than some other corporate environments; however as one leading UK-based client in the construction industry told us recently, they specifically wanted access to our case study for a top luxury London hotel because they were keen to achieve a level of customer service that replicates the standards of service in the luxury hotel market, and to add a level of personality that they had not focused on before. They added that, traditionally, the construction industry has not focused on this much-needed area of business and brand and they wanted to break the mould.

As Forrester suggests, create your own spreadsheets to show the difference it would make to your revenue if even 5 per cent more customers were to purchase again from you, or perhaps 10 per cent were to recommend your company to their contacts, resulting in a purchase. Creating a first-rate and consistent customer experience can have a significant impact on the bottom line.

You may think that this is obvious. However, in our work with large organizations around the world, we constantly find there is insufficient focus and appreciation of the real impact of a great customer experience. There is a general lack of effective employee training in this respect, particularly at customer touch-point level. Companies often provide customer-service training at these levels, but fail to reach the depths of what will make the difference to embedded behaviours. The level of understanding of what it is that I am expected to do and why it is important to me and the business is therefore missing. In addition, leaders and line managers are unaware of how to clearly promote and encourage the importance of living the brand with their teams. Yet arguably all this represents the biggest opportunity for business growth and increased market share facing organizations today.

We have to be mindful, however, that customer experience needs to be a *special* experience now in order for it to really make a difference. The bland and the basics are not enough anymore. As Shaun Smith from Smith+Co says, 'Price sensitivity has increased and it now takes a unique customer experience which goes beyond satisfaction and creates a real bond with the customer in order to regain the competitive edge' (Smith, 2010).

This book is intended to provide a thought-provoking look at how people behaviour could be diluting your corporate brand investment significantly more than you think. It sets out to provide some ways of measuring

FIGURE 0.4 The brand personality layer

this, and some options to address this potential imbalance. My content is based on several years of experience in helping organizations to improve the people brand element of their corporate brand and understanding their specific challenges. I will provide you with some insights into the brand problem and the gaps we face today in our businesses, common specific challenges via case studies and practical information from the Walking TALL Methodology to help you to implement some processes that will bridge the gap between your corporate brand and the one projected via your people. My intention is to provide a practical guide, to aid your awareness and thinking and the resulting strategic action so that all stakeholder experiences with your organization prove to be impactful, meaningful, consistent and in line with the corporate brand messages that you invest in so heavily.

I will provide, in some detail, the Walking TALL methodology for managing the people element of your brand and internalizing the values for individuals. Walking TALL has been utilized by many global organizations to motivate and engage their people to 'live the brand' and address challenges and imbalances. It is based on defining an individual's core authentic brand, refining that brand and packaging and projecting it effectively in a way that reinforces the corporate brand and values. The only way we can really get individuals to 'live the corporate brand' is by addressing the 'what's in it for me' factor and giving them something that they themselves can make sense of and utilize in their everyday lives and interactions, not just at work.

Summary

Corporate branding today is about more than it has been before. We have always had the corporate brand definition in the middle (example: Mercedes the brand); then customer experience at the next level with the specific product and the service (example: Mercedes SL 500 and its performance as the product, the car showroom, customer service etc). Now there is effectively another layer needed to maximize corporate brand investment – that of authentic people behaviour (the attitude of the car salesman, his interest in you the customer, his behaviours, etc) that will ultimately become more and more powerful in defining who your company is, what you stand for and whether I want to do business with you or not. This book addresses that additional external and critical layer – the personal brand of your people and the personality of your corporate brand. It looks at the considerations, refreshed focus and new practices needed to achieve the necessary balance in today's competitive and demanding business world.

References

Burns, M (2012) [accessed 7 October 2015] 'The state of customer experience, 2012' [Online] http://resources.moxiesoft.com/rs/moxiesoft/images/Forrester-The_State_Of_Customer_Experience_2012.pdf

Smith, S (2010) [accessed 7 October 2015] 'Customer experience and the numbers game' mycustomer 21 June. Available from: http://www.mycustomer.com/topic/customer-experience/shaun-smith-numbering-customer-experience/109345

Dilution of corporate values and loss of trust

01

In recent years there has been a steady decline in manners in business, leading to an almost accepted culture of apathy, rudeness, disrespect and general lack of common manners in communication and business dealings. All the good work often gets diluted and overpowered by the negative messages being projected. Sadly, it is the negative that gets remembered and talked about.

This chapter will look at the significant dilution that is happening with corporate brand investment, and the loss of trust that results. This is at a time when the brand-spend is increasing, particularly in digital marketing. Stephen Knight, CMO and group marketing director of SSE PLC in the United Kingdom says: 'SSE's search and digital display budgets have increased by over 100 per cent in the last year. Digital is now a major channel for us, driving better sales performance, connecting with our customers socially and building traffic to our websites. The trend is upwards as we seek to become digital first.'

With this clear focus in many businesses on connecting more with customers, we certainly need to see more of this spend allocated to the human elements of brand marketing in order to maximize the impact of the marketing budget.

Top brands that have traditionally relied upon their well-known name to carry them through, are finding that the name is no longer enough to maintain market share and sustain profits. Today, a greater intensity of positive customer experience is critical.

In this chapter, we'll be looking at:

- the impact of a deterioration in manners in business;
- loss of trust;
- the customer experience gap that is being created;

- bringing back trust and consistency;
- a global concern.

Where have all the manners gone?

In ongoing research with 120 professionals, managers and senior directors across several business sectors, we at Walking TALL have found that business communication in general is deteriorating. The basics of doing business have been diluted significantly during the past 10 years in particular, with a loss of focus on what is really important. It is becoming increasingly difficult to get that old culture of good customer service back and as a result we are heading towards an intolerable situation that may be irreversible if not addressed very soon.

Our research showed an incredible 73 per cent of people reporting an increase in poor communications and lack of respect in the workplace in the last five years. You would think with technology at our fingertips 24/7, that communication would be easier and more efficient. Our research shows that it's not; it's getting worse and it is in fact damaging our brands, both corporate and personal.

With regard to levels of responsiveness, we found 63 per cent of respondents agreeing that it is taking longer to receive responses to their communications (any form). This in turn can lead to a culture and mindset that 'if he doesn't respond, then I don't need to either'. This then snowballs. In addition, we found that over half of our respondents said they are experiencing an increase in colleagues cancelling meetings at short notice. Vast amounts of time are being wasted on chasing, checking, making excuses, unaccountability and the general extra workload created due to others not doing what they are meant to be doing.

What this suggests perhaps is that people are busier than ever. However, it also demonstrates that there is a lower level of respect for other people's time and efforts. We find that managers will pull team members from meetings or training courses in order to address 'something more urgent' without regard to the impact on the team member and their colleagues. Accountability expert Sam Silverstein says:

> Companies don't take time to determine what they believe in, therefore they don't communicate it, nor do they set absolute standards around it. So what happens is employees don't know how to act, don't know what the expectations are, and are not inspired to be accountable to each other.

In my experience, any apathetic internal culture like this leaks to the outside world and needs to be stopped in its tracks if we are to protect brand messages. Individuals in organizations often say to me, 'The way we interact with customers is different from how we behave internally when communicating with each other.' But in my experience – no it isn't!

As a result of all this, an attitude of distrust, unreliability and lack of responsibility slowly grows, when in fact in today's business world, customers and clients seek exactly the opposite. In the last three recessions, buying patterns have shown that our clients are searching not just for lower prices, but more for trust and the comfort that they are going to get what they pay for, including reliability and responsiveness. In the current climate, if our people are not delivering this then we are not only missing a huge opportunity for competitive advantage, we are also losing significantly large amounts of corporate brand investment, potential revenue and loyal customers.

The gap opening up

Your company and business brand today is about *people*. Corporate bad manners are entirely down to *people* behaviour, driven by many factors which we will explore in this book. In a climate where our clients want and need us to go the extra mile for a positive experience, with increased levels of communication, we can see a massive void about to open up.

How many times have you gone to a home improvement store, for example, expecting service and smiles just like the ones you've seen frequently on the latest TV advertising campaign, only to be disappointed in the actual reality of employee behaviours? Instead of the happy, energetic and upbeat employees you were expecting, you experience demotivation, apathy and a general lack of interest in their job. This does not suggest a cheerful and rewarding place to work! Company executives often say to me that they want to *exceed* the expectation of their customers; however, I believe that you only need to *meet* the expectation that is portrayed in your brand awareness and advertising. Doing this consistently will set you apart from your competitors and create customer loyalty – they know they are going to get what they expect to get.

Your organization will fall from a great height and make a huge dent in your brand reputation if your corporate culture is wrong. Furthermore, the trust in your service or product is diluted and loyalty among customers will start to suffer. This could be to a level from which it will be difficult, if not impossible, to recover for a long period of time. You may have got away with it so far in business, and traded off your previous successes and brand reputation; however, beware because this alone is unlikely to carry you through the next 10 years. You need consciously to work on closing the gap between the expectation you create through advertising and branding, and the experience your customers actually receive. Meeting expectations is required, not necessarily exceeding them.

'Meeting expectations is required, not necessarily exceeding them'

FIGURE 1.1   The sinkhole

The balance of supply and demand is out of kilter. The level or *supply* of corporate bad manners in the business world is increasing; at the same time the value placed on, or the *demand* for, a positive and unique customer experience is growing. Eventually the gap that is opened up creates a massive crater for a haemorrhaging of customer loyalty, positive social media hype, corporate brand investment and ultimately market share. We are more likely to be impacted by a bad customer experience, as we somehow have higher expectations that the experience will be good, perhaps due to heavy advertising, marketing messages and social media. Therefore when our expectations are not met, via the people interactions we have, then the gap is greater than it would have been should we not have had those expectations in the first place. To put this into context a little here – we're not necessarily talking about major, knock 'em dead experiences. I am referring in part to the simple things that cause us to remember a person, a situation or a company – a simple smile with eye contact, some interest shown in me, something that shows recognition of having met or spoken to me before and consistency – behaviours that create a feeling that we're valued as a customer. All these things can make a significant difference to how your stakeholders, including your customers, feel about you as a company. Moreover, they should be the simplest behaviours to project.

As bad customer experiences become more common, consumers are becoming less surprised by them. This opens up a huge opportunity for consumers to be delighted by a great customer experience and therefore to talk about it even more.

Feelings drive behaviours

People behaviour is ultimately affected by how they feel about themselves and how they are treated by others. If people are feeling valued, respected and empowered by colleagues and line managers for example, they will 'infect' others with similar positive behaviours. However, a lack of the same will create demotivation and disengagement and will be further compounded by too much to do, lack of training and limited career progression, which will likely result in a bad attitude. All these are contributing factors to corporate bad manners displayed externally as well as internally, affecting the behaviours of others around us and thereby compounding the issue. Of course, there are other factors to consider here too – such as rewards, workload and hours – that are beyond the scope of this book.

'Behaviours are ultimately affected by how we feel about ourselves'

FIGURE 1.2   The downward spiral

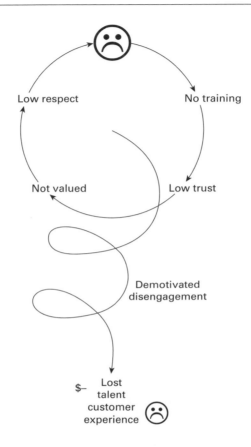

Loss of trust

So we can begin to see that the largely untapped resource within your corporate walls, that can build brand equity more effectively than you may have considered, is your people, and specifically those employees with strong and individual personal brands. It is these personal brands that can make your corporate brand real, trusted and pertinent in the eyes and minds of your customers and potential clients. This is because of the connection they bring and the human level of personality they add to the brand.

The corporate brand reputation you've been able to rely on and that your customers have trusted in previous decades, may not exist for much longer if the critical area of people brand is not addressed effectively now. Every

FIGURE 1.3   The upward spiral

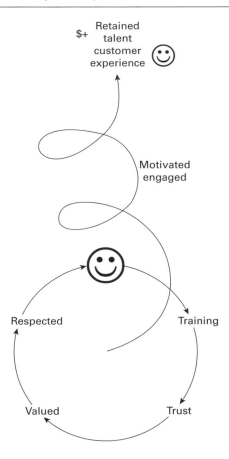

interaction adds a layer to your corporate brand and your reputation grows or declines as a result. This reputation is often created from the inside out, by the attitude of your people and how they feel about your company and the managers they report to. Customers move away from suppliers mostly due to perceived indifference. You rarely get to hear the specifics about how they feel undervalued, but your bottom line feels it.

The banking industry's reputation in particular has been in question in recent years and a loss of trust has occurred. Even though some of that reputation has been recovered, half of US adults say their trust in banks is still declining. Some 66 per cent of Americans state that personal experience with their banks has a great deal of influence on their level of trust (The Financial Brand, 2014). It is not easy to regain this trust once it has been broken.

CASE STUDY

I was interested in the Swedish bank Handelsbanken, who appear to have bypassed the typical fall in levels of trust in banks and have retained their customers' loyalty. They were ranked Europe's, and one of the world's, strongest banks (Bloomberg in 2013). Their model is one of localization – they give autonomy to their branches rather than operating at national or head office level, as they believe that each branch will know their local customers better than anybody else. They therefore allow their people to make decisions that are truly aligned to customers' needs, thus empowering the people who make the day-to-day decisions.

I interviewed Anders Bouvin, UK CEO of Handelsbanken UK. He is far from the traditional stereotype of the head of a bank. Anders first of all believes that customers ultimately control the brand of any organization – the brand is what your customers say it is. He says: 'Can you really talk about brand at all if the people are not aligned with what you say you are?' This belief is right at the heart of how Handelsbanken run their business. They are crystal clear in their communication of the bank's values and they keep it simple. Thousands of decisions are made every day and these are taken from the one core fundamental value they have at the bank – that of doing what is right for the customer at that time. Anders believes that many companies today say they put the customer first, but they do not have the energy or capacity to make this happen in reality. Many other banks have said they will replicate what Handelsbanken are doing, but they never actually achieve it. None has been able to achieve the radical change that is needed.

One of the key reasons Handelsbanken are able to really put their customers first is that they have eliminated all targets except the overall financial one, as they believe that any sort of product target can detract from doing what is best for the customer.

The important point here is that the core value of the company is simple, it is communicated clearly, and then processes are put in place to allow for every individual to adhere to that core value consistently.

Optimum brand management

FIGURE 1.4   The optimal corporate brand

The lines between the corporate brand and personal brand have always been a bit blurred. People say things like, 'My personal brand values are very different to those of the company and it would be wrong to change who I am just to fit in.' This is true. However, it really is quite simple – to gain the optimal projection of the corporate brand and maximize investment, you first need clarity on what you stand for as an organization in its most simple state. Then take people out of the corporate space, giving them time and tools to reflect on their personal brand and as such what these simple corporate values mean to them. By doing this you are encouraging them to interpret and internalize the values individually and inspiring them to modify behaviours in their everyday communications, being the best they can be. You then create this Yin and Yang between corporate and personal values that can otherwise sometimes appear not to correlate with each other.

Ultimately, you need to help your employees to build their personal brands in order to raise your corporate brand equity.

Measurement of people brand and behaviours

I have spoken to brand directors to gain an understanding of how much focus is put into measuring the actual effect of brand investment and how much of this effort, if any, is based on the human element of representation of the brand. As a result of this research, I found that there does seem to be a keen understanding of the importance of people behaviours on the success of brand messaging. However, I also found that in reality there is not enough being worked through strategically with learning and development to get to the deep levels needed to affect the necessary engagement levels. Nor is there effective measurement in place. In later chapters we will explore what is missing and what some companies are using in order to reach the required levels.

Sarah Dickins, executive people director of Friends Provident, believes that in the past, businesses' brands have not been recognized as playing as important a role as they do now. She says: 'When there are strengths in the customer base, the perception has been that we don't need to focus on brand as much. That's now changed.' At Friends Provident they do seem to understand the importance of the links between brand and people and they have robust systems in place to support this belief. We'll hear more about how they are addressing this in later chapters.

CASE STUDY

Some organizations do manage to achieve a high level of consistency with their customer experience. John Lewis is a chain of upmarket department stores throughout the United Kingdom, with 23,000 partners (as they call employees). I interviewed Andrew Murphy, board retail director of John Lewis, and he believes that their biggest success factors in achieving this level of consistency are in recruiting the right people and then in putting their partners first. He says, 'The single biggest focus for us is our partners' happiness. This is a focus from the chairman down.' Their number one commercial focus is the customer, but their partners are number one to them. 'It might be more logical or fashionable to put customers first, but in order to genuinely achieve what the customer wants and needs, you have to do something, which on the surface is counter-intuitive and place them second.'

John Lewis's recruitment process is managed 100 per cent internally and they don't involve agencies. They also have in place what they call 'Time with the Team'. This involves a potential candidate for a role, following an initial interview, spending some time with the actual team they would be working with. This process allows them to uncover behavioural elements that they wouldn't be able to in a formal interview and helps them to be so successful in recruiting the right people.

In addition, when asked about the happiness factor they focus on, I discovered that they constantly monitor this by a group of peer-selected partners' meetings each month to discuss what is and isn't working. The findings are regularly reported back to the retail director and most importantly they are addressed. There is no measure attached to this process, but because partners know it is in place they are more consistent with and conscious of their behaviours. 'Partners feel they are listened to and heard, and therefore valued for what they do in their role', says Andrew Murphy.

John Lewis also focus heavily on relevant training programmes that provide partners with 'a route to identify and understand themselves in the context of that bigger and potentially distant brand message'. They have a training programme called 'Love to Sell', which has sub-modules called 'Love to Serve', 'Love to Solve', etc. These are part behaviour-focused, part psychology and part technical skills. The programmes are closely linked to the brand messaging and they serve to keep partners in touch in a relevant way with what the business aims for and stands for.

However, in publicly quoted businesses, the challenge that arises is sustaining this level of training investment and management when the business is subject to quarterly pressures on results and profit and loss. It is still crucial that a level of investment is retained for keeping employees engaged. The negative impact on consistent customer experience is too great without it.

As an executive or person of influence in your company, it's time to stop paying lip-service to customer experience, or just simply talking about 'living the brand', and instead start measuring the effect people behaviour is having on your corporate brand investment and do something strategic about it. It's not only a threat to your business but also a major opportunity to stand out, stand up and be different, creating a magnet for customers and clients, and a story for them to shout about. After all, people love to talk about positive experiences and recommend something they have experienced to their friends and business colleagues.

Right from the outset

The first impression you make has never been more important than it is in business today. We live in a very visual, image-conscious and fast-moving world, where that vital first impression is made in seconds. In fact, a study at Princeton University by Alexander Todorov, illustrated that we make a first impression in one-tenth of a second (Todorov and Willis, 2006). Whether it's 10 seconds or less, the fact is that we never get a second chance to make that impression. It can take many more experiences with a person to change a first impression and often in business we don't get that opportunity if it's a negative one. Harvard Business School social psychologist, Amy

Cuddy, says that when meeting someone for the first time, we form not one impression, but two. 'We're judging how warm and trustworthy the person is, and that's trying to answer the question, "What are this person's intentions toward me?" And we're also asking ourselves, "How strong and competent is this person?"' (Capps, 2012). Her research shows that these two traits, trustworthiness and confidence, account for 80 to 90 per cent of first impressions.

When we meet somebody for the first time, we will take in the non-verbal communication first of all – the dress, appearance and body language. Then when they start to speak, we take in the clarity, credibility and impact of the voice. From what we see and how we hear it, we decide in seconds whether they are worth listening to or not. We will then hook into the content more effectively, or not as the case may be.

Think of those times when you've been at a corporate conference and the speaker, perhaps the head of finance, comes on stage and says, 'Sorry I've not prepared for today so I hope it goes OK.' What are you likely to be thinking at this point? You certainly won't have confidence in what they are about to share with you. Then they proceed to compound this poor opening by reading directly from slides so their voice isn't projected into the audience clearly. This weak and uninspiring style continues throughout the 40 minutes of the presentation, creating a significant negative layer to their brand and ultimately that of the company. It suggests in the minds of the audience, a lack of respect reflected in poor preparation, lack of self-awareness and lack of coaching to present an inspiring message. Business leaders today have no excuse for not presenting well – there are many opportunities to improve presentation skills and stage presence and we will cover some more on this in Chapter 7, Presentational Brand. It is a necessary skill that you are expected to master.

Halo or horns

We can also associate a 'halo or horns' effect with first impressions. If you have a positive impression of somebody during the initial stages of a conversation for example, what you tend to do is subconsciously pick up on other positive things about that person as the conversation goes on. Then you also 'hear' positive things about them from other people and your impression is confirmed. The same happens with a negative first impression – you will subconsciously search for other negative elements you hear or read about them and the impression is reinforced. The lesson to be taken away is to bring your first impression to your conscious radar, rather than leaving it in the depths of oblivion.

A global concern

This apparent lack of appreciation for the significant power and opportunity that the people behaviour element of the corporate brand represents is not just happening in isolated countries or industries. From our international work and experience, we find this deterioration of effective communication in the corporate world happening in other parts of the globe, across all sectors, to varying degrees. Furthermore, different cultures dictate a different level of people behaviour and therefore customer experience and this fact alone could have a significant impact on doing business globally. Creating a consistency of experience becomes even more difficult when our businesses span several global geographical areas. For example, I find when dealing with some Latin American countries, a lack of or slow communication or acknowledgement of a communication is commonplace in their culture and it is not considered disrespectful to others. However, to other cultures outside of Latin America, this type of behaviour could become significantly detrimental to doing business. Germans and northern Europeans tend to be very exacting and responsive. If we connect Germans with Latin Americans you can see the perceptions that can be created and the potential damage to business relations as a result.

While we cannot and should not attempt to change global cultures, we do need to be mindful of the differences and appreciate the added need for establishing corporate values and ensuring that they are fully understood, taken on-board and reinforced by all individuals every day, wherever they are in the world.

It appears therefore that this is a global business concern, as companies continue to expand across international and cultural borders. However, at the same time, it is a perfect opportunity to stand out and for your corporate brand to be remembered for all the right reasons.

Moving forwards

The important realization in this chapter is the significant gap that is now growing rapidly between customer expectations and the actual experience they receive and ultimately talk about. People behaviours are becoming generally more apathetic, and while there is a recognition that this is the case, very few companies are putting in the required energy and resources to address it really effectively.

Use this as the starting point for change, and as we work through the following chapters you can begin to put the 'meat on the bones' to form a strategy to activate positive behavioural change in your individuals, teams and leadership, and ultimately shift to an enhancement in culture in terms of trust and respect, internally and externally.

References

Capps, R (2012) [accessed 7 October 2015] 'First impressions: the science of meeting People' Wired, 20 November. Available from: www.wired.com/2012/11/amy-cuddy-first-impressions/

The Financial Brand (2014) [accessed 7 October 2015] 'Why are Americans losing trust in banks (again)?' 11 November. Available from: http://thefinancialbrand.com/44896/customer-trust-banking-industry/

Todorov, A and Willis, J (2006) [accessed 7 October 2015] 'First impressions: Making up your mind after a 100-ms exposure to a face' *Psychological Science*, July. Available from: http://pss.sagepub.com/content/17/7/592.short?rss=1&ssource=mfc

Your brand from all angles

02

Your corporate brand will be portrayed by many factors and some of those quite possibly areas that you haven't considered as part of the branding strategy. In fact, important areas of brand can also be overlooked during your efforts to engage all employees with the brand messaging. This chapter will look at how your brand is projected from all angles and help you to bring some of the less obvious areas back under your control from a consistent messaging viewpoint. It includes:

- 'old-style' branding and why it's no longer enough;
- hidden elements of brand messaging;
- internal culture;
- third-party danger zones;
- communication is king.

Corporate branding today is mostly about multiple stakeholders interacting with your brand, and its success therefore is largely dependent on your employees' attitudes and behaviours in delivering the brand promise. Your brand image as a company creates expectations from all of your stakeholders. It defines who you are, how you operate, and how you are different from your competitors. Your brand image is a promise that you must keep and are expected to keep, and whether the positioning of your brand is successful or not remains in the hands of your employees and their behaviours.

The end result or the customer experience is the fulfilment of that promise or guarantee. This experience cannot be left to chance and it should be consciously and continually monitored, managed and controlled in alignment with the image you want to project. It therefore needs to reinforce the brand messages consistently across every touch-point. Every person who directly or indirectly has an impact on the customer experience is a key player. Service brands in particular remain vulnerable because of their reliance on your employees. Your brand image and brand investment is at risk if your brand promise or guarantee is not fulfilled, and it will not be easy to get it back on-track.

The traditional approach is not enough

Typically in a re-brand process, you bring in a brand agency to create a brand and work on how that brand is projected in the traditional ways, such as advertising, sponsorship and product packaging. In addition, sometimes brand experience specialists are hired to assess, create and address the full customer experience element too. Both are much-needed services and well worth the investment. However, this alone is no longer enough.

There is often more resource applied to these 'non-human' elements than those areas that really create the memory of the brand in the customers' eyes; the personality of the brand projected via the interaction they have with the people in your organization. Frequently, executive teams do not pay enough attention to just how powerfully their corporate brand is projected to the outside world by people alone, both positively and negatively. I have spoken to many CEOs and directors of large organizations on this point, and they will verbally agree wholeheartedly that this is crucial to the bottom line and market share. However, all too often customer service training programmes still focus on the transactional elements of customer service rather than the authentic and outstanding experience that goes beyond the expected, that we want and need the customer to go away with and talk about. This all-important experience will inevitably come from the softer skills, emotional intelligence and natural intuition of the member of staff in assessing a situation to influence thinking and subsequent behaviour. I often speak to companies where they will tell me they have spent hundreds of thousands of dollars on their 'new look' brand or new customer facility, and yet when it comes to gaining budget approval for the real personality of the brand training – the element that will ultimately make the real difference and that drives the results – inevitably the budget is not there and is often not found. It's akin to designing and building a fabulous new sports car and not putting an engine in it!

In addition, even if the people-behaviour element of the brand is addressed to the level it should be for client-facing front-line staff, it is rarely in my experience considered as important for those members of staff who work in the 'back office' functions such as IT, administration support, legal departments and accounts payable. These people are considered not to be client facing and, therefore, they are often overlooked when it comes to customer service or behavioural training programmes. This is a potentially dangerous oversight.

Making the brand stick at all levels

It's essential for employees at all levels of your company – from the senior leadership team to your most junior member of staff, to understand the big-picture view of the customer experience and the overall corporate objective. What makes it really stick for them is if they can see the specific brand touch-points that they carry out every day and how this all fits into the overall goal. This is critical not just for front-line staff, but is as important for back-office employees who often believe they have no impact on the customer experience. Making the connection for them, to help them to see that what they do behind the scenes in their everyday roles has as much impact on the customer experience as what their front-line colleagues do, is crucial for consistency of brand.

Today every single touch-point becomes as important as the next in providing building blocks that get talked about as a consistent brand experience. Your team members in the back-office areas of your business could seriously dilute all the great things being done at the front end of customer service, if they are not on-board with the brand messaging and understand what it truly means to the same extent. If in their role they cannot easily appreciate the big picture and brand objective and the part they play, then a significant gap could appear in the overall experience of your customers, stakeholders and suppliers. Consider the effect of a poor billing process, or a CRM system that fails to record information consistently, or even the legal department giving advice to a supplier-facing employee that shows little appreciation of the reality of the supplier situation or needs.

It's worth remembering that your clients also have their own customers to service. If their life is made difficult because of complex processes and jobsworth mindsets within your organization, that means that their customers in turn could be provided with a less than satisfactory service, and they will likely leave you. Brand reputation is affected by many areas of your business, and significantly so in apparently invisible areas too.

Back-office processes and people are just as important as your front-line customer service employees and systems when it comes to your brand reputation. If your employees are able to put themselves in the shoes of your customers or suppliers, and consider how their behaviour and internal processes can make the customers' or suppliers' lives as easy as possible, then you achieve greater consistency with the experience provided. You can only achieve this level of appreciation with the right training and the right internal environment and culture to encourage it.

Understanding of the customer experience helps everybody in your organization to see your company as your customers do. For companies to win the loyalty of devotion of their customers, they need to experience their brands from the outside in.

Peter Cheese, CEO of the Chartered Institute of Personnel and Development (CIPD) in the United Kingdom, told me that he believes in order for individuals to be fully immersed and engaged in reinforcing the corporate brand, there also has to be alignment. 'Individuals need to be, not just engaged but aligned to the purpose, outcomes and objectives. They can be engaged but this could be in the wrong direction.' This is an interesting consideration – are you really measuring true engagement and alignment to the brand, or just engagement per se?

Individuals need to be able to see how what they do specifically in their role relates to the overall corporate or team objectives. What purpose do they fulfil?

In order to effectively engage people to the level needed for them to be their best and do their best at work, you need to consider three core elements:

1 Empowerment
2 Support
3 Purpose

Empowerment

Most people have the ability to make the right decisions but have been stifled by their direct line manager. An individual needs to feel valued and respected for the role they do and what they bring to the overall team objective in order to get on with the job in hand and operate to their full potential. Every individual has an inner drive and this needs to be exploited to allow their full potential to be reached. I believe that everybody wants to come to work with the intention of doing the best job they can, but they need the environment and encouragement to enable this.

Support

It's not enough just to say that you empower people to make the right decisions; you also need to support this actively to give them the confidence to operate in this manner. You and your line managers throughout the business have a responsibility to help them to develop and progress. Generation Y and Z will also expect and demand this level of support, so it's no longer an option to ignore it.

Purpose

People need to understand why they are doing something and what difference it makes to end results. Without a clear purpose or direction, none of us is inspired to work hard to make a difference and influence change.

These three core components should be part of your everyday agenda with your employees. Added to this, employees need to be given the tools to develop their own personal brands encompassing these core elements. The complete combination of these four areas provides you with true engagement of your staff. When we look at personal brands in Chapter 5, we will address in more depth the challenge of allowing people to be their best selves authentically.

FIGURE 2.1   True engagement

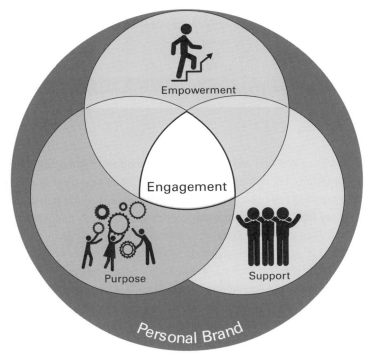

= True Engagement

Your brand to suppliers

Today, it is not only consumers who have a choice of who to buy from. As suppliers we also have a choice on who we want to work with or partner with. In an age when people are focused more on positive energy, wellbeing and good life balance, there is more of a tendency to adopt the 'life is too short' way of thinking and avoid the unnecessary negative factors where possible. Therefore in a business-to-business company, if you are difficult to work with, you may find that not only do good suppliers not want to work with you, but that they will be more likely to talk about their negative experience to their professional colleagues too.

Your suppliers usually run businesses themselves of course, with their own set of customers and stakeholders. It's worth noting that they can become brand ambassadors for you, given a consistent and positive experience of working with your company from all angles. Or, of course, can equally speak negatively about you to their network.

As a supplier I find that when dealing with back-office departments, often people either just do what they need to do to 'do their job', or fall short of what they need to do. There can often be little apparent appreciation for the fact that they are an important part of the company brand too. I frequently experience a lack of accountability, responsibility, seeing through an issue to conclusion, or general collaboration and teamwork compared with their colleagues in more front-line roles.

CASE STUDY

Our team had been working with the head of learning and development for a large global organization on defining a suitable personal branding and executive presence programme for senior managers. Walking TALL was the solution they wanted and we had finally got to a stage of rollout. Through this whole process, the communication was professional, consistent, responsive and very respectful on both sides.

Then it came to dealing with the accounts payable department when the first invoice was submitted. A whole new relationship scenario was experienced. In fact, it was like dealing with a completely different company and set of corporate values. Had these people gone through a totally separate induction process into the organization? Or perhaps they had received no training on corporate values at all? Communication ceased. First, we couldn't get a response from them to confirm that the invoice was in their system. When it became overdue, we still could not elicit a response. We have a process that we go through in our business when invoices are not paid, but we prefer to have a voice-to-voice conversation and establish what the issue might be before going down the route of issuing late payment invoices. When we finally did get a response to messages and e-mails, the people involved (and yes, there were several) consistently didn't do what they said they would do and had to be chased at every communication point.

Now a repetitive attitude of unaccountability and unresponsiveness like this is no coincidence, nor is it isolated – it is indicative of a culture in that department, and possibly in a wider part of the company. In fact a culture of blame is often apparent in these situations. Not a great brand message to project to the outside world and we find it is sadly all too common.

This, of course, had the effect of completely tainting our view of that company's brand. Unfortunately, this is the brand we remembered rather than the more positive one that we had consistently experienced with the heads of learning and development and human resources. The experience that causes the most pain is the one that sticks with us. Of course, this is one that also gets talked about and potentially written about! It would be a worthwhile exercise to find out what your suppliers feel and say about your company to their contacts – why not ask them?

Internal culture

This type of culture that breeds within a team or department, or sometimes even company-wide, is described well by Steve Simpson, creator of UGRs – Unwritten Ground Rules. UGRs, he says, can best be described with this example of an employee's mindset, as one of many:

> The company talks about good customer service, but we know they don't really mean it, so we don't really have to worry about it. (Simpson, 2015)

Another could be:

> Nobody else bothers to respond to or speak to suppliers chasing invoices, so why should I?

Often, of course, these ways of thinking are subconscious for the individual involved, and that's what sadly builds the culture. People tend to copy or subconsciously reflect or mirror the behaviours of others without thinking. It then becomes a habit and the attitude of 'it's just the way things are done around here' starts to stick. How about the employee who always turns up to work late? If this appears not to be dealt with by management, it will certainly encourage a culture of apathy among others about time keeping and resentment towards that member of staff. Could this be true of your organization? Do you really check?

As Steve Simpson says, 'It is the UGRs that drive people's behaviour – incredibly, these are rarely, if ever, discussed openly' (Simpson, 2015).

In another example, we had developed a very positive relationship with the business development director of a small business consultancy, and were focused on jointly developing and delivering a successful programme to one of their clients. All was going very well indeed. Again, when it got to dealing with other members of staff, in this case within the legal department of the business regarding the contract, things went downhill rapidly. It was again like dealing with a different company and with people who had a completely incongruent perspective on what the company values were. In this instance, we chose to pull out of this business partnership due entirely to the mismatch of values with our own and the inconsistency of staff behaviours in the back office. The trust had disappeared, so it was not going to work long term.

The inconsistencies in these types of experiences are precisely where companies need to place focus and attention. If an experience is not consistent, it causes us as suppliers or customers to question the integrity of the company and we start to mistrust. This also serves to dramatically dilute all the great work that your front-line employees do to build effective and positive relationships that get talked about. Unfortunately, the only thing talked about now is the negative behaviours, which spread, across social media too.

You may have a focus on communicating the *customer brand promise*, and the attitudes and behaviours expected from employees to deliver on that promise, especially customer-facing staff. While it is clearly beneficial to the organization for employees to understand their responsibilities in delivering the customer brand promise, the effectiveness of initiatives to reinforce this can often be short-lived if the brand values on which the service experience is founded are not experienced internally by the employees in their interactions with the organization.

TripAdvisor – a trust indicator

In the hospitality and retail industries, TripAdvisor is widely relied upon by consumers to assess the quality of a product or service. Yelp has a wider reach outside of just retail and hospitality. They both have a huge impact on purchasing behaviour. I don't know about you, but I always look for the negative comments first before I really consider going to or experiencing that particular service or venue. Yes, the positive ones reinforce; but the negative ones certainly cause me not to try that company. As media and corporate reputation coach, Alan Stevens says:

> There are three ways in which potential customers learn about companies:
>
> **1** Paid – traditional print and broadcast advertising, Google and Facebook adverts
>
> **2** Owned – websites, brochures
>
> **3** Earned – review sites and social media.
>
> In terms of trust and decision-making, it is the third of these that now holds sway. There is far less trust in what companies or their PR and advertising agencies say, than in the views of former and existing customers.

Alan goes on to say, 'There is only one thing that customers write reviews about, and that is customer service. There is no product or service good enough to overcome a bad customer experience.'

The experience that gets written about will *always* come from, or at the very least be influenced by an interaction with a person or a people experience. I recently took friends to a very pleasant-looking outdoor restaurant/bar in my home town. I had been there before, a couple of years previously and received average service. However, I decided to try it again as the surroundings were welcoming this particular evening. After only 10 minutes, we experienced slow and unfriendly service and a less-than-cheerful waitress who made us feel like we were an inconvenience. We stayed, but left much sooner than we would have done, had the service been in line with what the restaurant seemed to offer from the outside.

Needless to say, I added a TripAdvisor review about the negative service experience we had. It was nothing to do with the food or the environment, which were both good. But the overall experience was so badly tainted by the service that it wouldn't have mattered to me how good the product – I will not be going back again. I would guess that a number of other people will also avoid going due to reading the review.

Consumers will be driven to express their views on TripAdvisor or Yelp when the experience differs either positively or negatively from what they expected. While I try to keep a good balance between good and bad reviews, respondents who suffered a bad interaction are 50 per cent more likely to share it on social media (not just TripAdvisor or Yelp, but Twitter, Facebook and so on too) than those who had good experiences (MarketingCharts, 2013). The same survey shows that 54 per cent of respondents who had shared a bad experience said they shared it more than five times, compared to 33 per cent of those who had shared a good interaction.

The important point here is that customer experience has superseded the quality of the product for causing consumers to talk about that product. Customers write good reviews when something happens to make them feel good, therefore this should give you a good indication of what needs to be addressed and considered. Furthermore, it is an excellent opportunity to improve your ratings online and how people talk about you to their contacts, directly and via social media.

Responding to bad as well as good reviews should be a strategic process followed in your organization – it's another great opportunity to express your true qualities as a company and goes a long way to diluting a negative comment. No response at all suggests that you really don't care and we know that apathy can lead to lost customers.

In our work with Grosvenor House, a JW Marriott hotel in London, we learned just how much emphasis is put on having a great customer experience and how this can be effectively monitored in part by independent travel websites.

The guest satisfaction survey (also known as Guest Voice) within Marriott hotels is combined with other feedback from websites like TripAdvisor and Booking.com, by an external company to create another metric, Brand Karma. This provides benchmarking with their competitor hotels.

Interestingly in addition, Grosvenor House metrics for 'satisfactory' guest experience have now been raised from 8 to 9, with 9 or 10 being deemed satisfactory and anything below not being counted. Therefore, standards of excellence have been raised.

This seems to be indicative of trends in many service-driven industries – the levels of expectation are rising and possibly at a time when standards are falling.

FIGURE 2.2 Raised standards of excellence

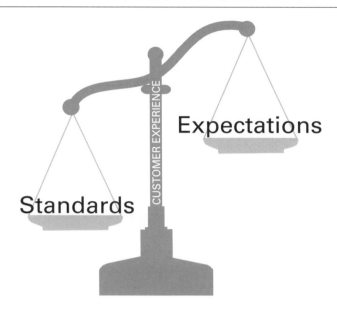

CUSTOMER EXPERIENCE

Expectations

Standards

CASE STUDY

A few years ago, I was delivering a personal branding programme for the management team at the Langham Hotel, one of London's five-star luxury hotels. On Day One I had lunch in the restaurant with the HR director. On the drinks menu I quickly spotted one of my favourite soft drinks that I grew up with, and you don't see that often on menus – ginger beer. So I ordered my ginger beer with great enthusiasm and a vision of a long, cool, iced drink with a slice of lime – it would of course be presented beautifully at the Langham Hotel. However, a few minutes later, the waiter returned looking a little uncomfortable and said: 'I'm so sorry, madam, we don't have any ginger beer today.' Massive disappointment of course, but we had a bit of a laugh about the expectation being shattered.

My car had been valet-parked for the duration of the two-day programme. When my car was brought back to me, on the passenger seat there was a bottle of ginger beer and a note that said 'Enjoy', and a bottle opener so I could have it on the way home. Wow, what an impact that made on me! However, it didn't end there. Four months later I had organized a conference in London and brought some international speaker friends over. We all stayed at the Langham Hotel. You can guess what was in my room when I checked in that night – yes, two bottles of ginger beer on ice, and a note that said 'Enjoy'.

The reason of course that this had such an impact on me was because it related to me personally, and it created an experience I would certainly remember and talk about. I have told this story in many keynotes around the world, to many thousands of people and I know it makes an impact and gets remembered because I often get cards, pictures, photos and even gifts of ginger beer sent through the mail to me, referring to the Langham Hotel experience.

One of the Langham Hotel's strongest values is providing exceptional customer service. Mike the waiter certainly achieved it for me that day and provided an experience that was special and remembered and went beyond my expectations.

Yet again, another great example of my belief that the most valuable part of your brand today is what your customers and clients say about your brand to their contacts.

The other important aspect of this story is that the Langham Hotel has created an environment that allowed and empowered the waiter to make a decision himself to do this, communicate this to his colleagues in valet service and then update this on the CRM system for four months later. Do you truly empower and encourage your staff to make decisions that are right for your customers at the time, and furthermore do you recognize them for it? Luxury standards are almost the easy bit – it's going to that next level of excellence that takes thought, intuition and a degree of customer focus beyond the norm.

Anders Bouvin, CEO of Handelsbanken in the United Kingdom, says: 'People tend to blossom when they are empowered. Recruit the right people and treat them like grown-ups. Respect them – they know their customers best.'

As consumers and business people, we are constantly looking now to ensure that we get 'what we pay for', rather than necessarily the cheapest option. This is due to our desire to 'trust' a product, service or company, more so than ever before. We feel we need to know that the company has personality, is authentic, not just full of great words and promises. They need to live and breathe the values via their people across all disciplines in the organization.

FIGURE 2.3   Extended brand influence

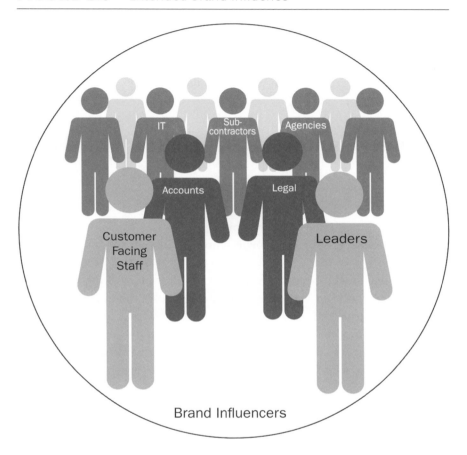

Third-party danger zones

With the increase in outsourcing of certain departments such as the whole supply chain, customer support and third-party sales agents, there is a greater potential for your company brand values to be severely diluted. The task of trying to align sub-contracted employees to your brand is a tough one. First, I would ask if you are measuring the impact of sub-contractor staff behaviours on your customers and are you even sure you are getting accurate feedback? Sometimes customers just move away to another supplier and you never know why or were never aware there was a potential problem in the first place. In fact, more customers will move to an alternative supplier because of indifference experienced from their current supplier, not necessarily from bad service. One unfortunate customer experience offers a supplier a great opportunity to truly demonstrate their corporate brand values and to prove that one situation might just have been a blip rather than the norm. How a negative situation is dealt with can very often turn out to be a fabulous opportunity to regain the loyalty of those customers.

You never quite know when your brand is on show

I recall one particular experience while at an exhibition. We were hosting a booth for our training company and opposite was the booth of a well-known insurance group. The female representative on the booth was not presented in a way that I would have expected from this particular company. She also looked bored, was indifferent to people walking past, didn't engage in conversation with them and was generally the opposite of what I would have expected. In a quiet moment I went over to speak to her. During our conversation, she told me that she didn't actually work for the company she was representing on the booth; she worked for an agency. I couldn't help wondering what sort of checks were in place by this insurance company as to the staff being used to portray their brand in such a public way. In fact, I did write a constructive letter to the managing director to mention that he might want to be aware of this potential brand dilution, and received a reply to say they were perfectly happy with their contractor and the way their brand was being projected by them.

On the other hand, when living in the United Kingdom, every week we would use our regular grocery home delivery from our favourite supermarket, Tesco. Every week it was a different delivery driver, but each one of them was consistently cheerful (whatever the weather), helpful, chatty and above all had a great authentic personal brand. Tesco employ their own 'customer delivery assistants' rather than sub-contract to another company, so they can lead and develop the way they behave much more effectively. I interviewed Mark Chapman, Tesco's customer fulfilment centre's director, to find out how they achieve this level of consistency. First, Mark told me that he has a vision of a 'great place to work, and iconic service' in the Tesco fulfilment operation. They don't just pay lip-service to this vision with the customer delivery team, they work exceptionally hard to ensure that each and every driver feels this in their everyday experiences working at Tesco. For example, they give them a great fulfilment centre environment to work from, with personal lockers, good food and a high-quality uniform. The group leader's first response to requests for leave is always 'yes', even if it's going to take some working through to make it possible. In short, they treat their drivers well and demonstrate at each opportunity that they value them. What they demand in return is that the drivers look after their customers exceptionally well. Of course, this has a tendency to happen organically as the drivers are looked after so well as employees.

Tesco ask their drivers to bring their personality to work – they want them to be authentic and project their personal brands. This certainly comes across, as you will know if you've ever experienced Tesco grocery home deliveries. Overall, a great business model, that seems to work incredibly well. Of course, this type of culture is more difficult to achieve across an entire organization. However, it is possible if we can empower all employees to be authentic and be the best they can be, starting with creating an environment that inspires, nurtures and provides for this.

Some supermarket chains and other retail outlets use sub-contractors for their delivery service of course. A recent experience with a clothing manufacturer demonstrated for me how badly wrong this can go. They consistently failed to deliver the product ordered and did not communicate, so that in the end I gave up and cancelled the order. My desire to buy from this particular brand again is zero. This is nothing to do with the service from the company themselves or the product, but purely down to their third-party delivery service. I don't need to state which piece of the experience will be remembered and talked about. I'm sure you've had similar experiences. What a dilution and waste of brand investment. In fact in this particular case, when I did speak to management to explain the situation, I was told they were well aware of the issues with the third-party courier service but had been told they could do nothing about it. How bizarre that a company that spends millions of pounds on their marketing and branding, would be so relaxed about the most relevant customer touch-point in their business – that of the physical interaction between them and their customer, at their own home.

CASE STUDY

A few years ago one of our clients was a company called Water for Work and Home (now part of Water Wellbeing Group) – a medium-sized business in the south of England. Their business provides delivery of water to homes and offices around the United Kingdom. They recognized early on in our discussions about a company-wide focus on the people element of the brand, that their delivery drivers – or their Water Men as they call them – were quite simply the most important people in their business. They represented the most valuable customer touch-point for them. As such, we put together a specific and tailored programme for this group of people that focused on them as brand ambassadors and made them feel valued as the focal part of the business, rather than 'just the van drivers'. The management team recognized early on that their brand could be seriously enhanced or indeed damaged by this group of people alone. They are very particular about who they recruit into these important roles and with our programme gave them the training they needed in areas of their brand that included conversational skills, dress and appearance and self-awareness as brand ambassadors. They are now one of the United Kingdom's largest and most successful independent suppliers of water coolers and bottled water, and it all started as a small family-run business back in 1992. Their website talks about Water Men on the home page and says: 'Our Water Men are at the very heart of our business. In fact, they're our eyes and ears too!' What a mantra to have!

At the other end of the corporate scale, we had an exceptional demonstration of corporate values from the CEO/founder himself. I won't mention the name of the company in this book; however, I regularly mention this story to friends and colleagues and recommend the company as a result of what happened to me. This company states on their website that they are 'Trusted all over the World'. A strong brand statement to make and live up to. They had messed up part of their service that I had booked with them and the potential consequences were looking a little dire. I posted a comment on Twitter in a desperate attempt to get a solution to the problem. At that point the CEO himself picked this up and realized that he was in a position to help us – and he did. The problem was solved in less than 30 minutes. This situation went from one of never using them again and writing about it, to complete trust that even though they made a mistake (and of course it happens), they live and breathe their values and will handle any situation appropriately for the client. I'm now, of course, a total champion of their company and brand. If we ever meet, ask me who they are and I'll tell you! It'll also prove that you read my book.

If the CEO is setting the example, there is a better chance that the rest of the leadership team, line managers and every employee will 'get' the culture and what is expected of them. It then becomes a situation of 'that's the way things are done around here', and a standard is set.

How does your business measure up?

So here are some questions to consider for your organization to enable you to assess if you are addressing all angles of your brand reputation:

1 Do you invest proportionate amounts of resource in the hard element of your corporate brand (advertising, sponsorship, logos etc), and the softer people behaviour elements? Is the weighting justified?

2 Do you truly know where your most valuable customer touch-points are and maximize their impact?

3 Do you effectively measure how your customers and *suppliers* feel about their complete brand experience with you?

4 What measures do you have in place to ensure that your managers and staff are fully engaged with the values and portraying them through their behaviours every day?

5 Are you gaining enough feedback from customers and stakeholders in parts of your business where third parties are involved?

6 Are you checking how third parties and sub-contractors are representing your brand? Do they feel a part of your brand?

7 Are you encouraging a feedback culture?

8 If you're gaining all the feedback, what are you doing with it?

9 Have you considered a reward system for providing great stakeholder experience?

10 Is social media impact being effectively monitored, measured and acted upon?

Recognizing the value of feedback

Question 8 – about what you're doing with the feedback – is crucial. How many times have you completed a survey as a consumer or client with negative comments and yet have received no follow-up to gain more information from you? What an opportunity missed by the company to fully understand where the customer experience is not on message, to put measures in place to correct it and ultimately create the experience that gets talked about for positive reasons.

I recently went to great lengths to provide constructive feedback for a house rental agency I used. In fact they persisted in sending me the questionnaire to complete. The service I had received was far from acceptable and professional, but I felt it would be useful, notwithstanding my limited free time, to give the company accurate feedback so they could look into where they might improve. My feedback was wide open to further discussion and I even offered to discuss it with them; but yes you've guessed, not even an acknowledgement let alone a follow-up call was forthcoming. I can only assume that companies like this are ignorant of the fact that this level of apathy will result in losing customers today on a bigger scale than ever before due to the spread of negative messages quicker than they can imagine. In fact, this level of service I have found is consistent in the estate and rental agency business in the United Kingdom in particular. So if you manage a business in this area, please seize the opportunity to stand out from your competitors and change the unfortunate stereotypical image of this industry.

> Apathy loses customers

Communication is king

Perhaps today the phrase 'communication is king' is as important as 'the customer is king' was a few years ago (and is still considered so by some). However, the focus has shifted – if we get all the channels of communication in alignment with the brand messages, then ultimately the customer will benefit anyway. Richard Branson is well known for saying he puts staff first above the customer. He believes that if you treat your staff well, they are happy and therefore will create better experiences for your customers. Similarly, one unhappy employee can ruin the brand experience not just for one, but for numerous customers.

Simple really, and of course it appears to work for Virgin. Branson has said he can't believe more companies don't operate in this way. In an interview for my book *Walking TALL* he told me, 'If the person who works at your company is not appreciated, they are not going to do things with a smile.' In not treating employees well, companies risk losing customers over bad service. With this in mind, Branson says he has made sure that Virgin prioritizes employees first, customers second and shareholders third. 'Effectively, in the end shareholders do well, the customers do better, and your staff remains happy,' he says.

What Branson is effectively saying here is that if your staff are communicated with well, understand the values of the company clearly, are valued and respected, then you get the best attitude from them. That gets passed onto your customers. We now live in an age where communication and interaction between managers, the leadership team and employees is of paramount importance to success. Effective communication strengthens the connection between a company and all of its stakeholders – those people affected in some way by the company's actions: customers, employees, shareholders, suppliers, and the community. When communication breaks down, the results can be anything from time wasting to disastrous.

I found with our Walking TALL research with managers and directors in large organizations that sadly communication levels and standards are decreasing, often resulting in an environment of mistrust and ambiguity. If people are not communicated with effectively, meaning that they don't interpret the message in the way the person delivering it intended, then messages are left wide open to misperception. For example, we found that people are taking longer to respond to e-mails. This may be interpreted as 'not having got the message', 'can't be bothered to reply to the message', 'don't have the answer to the message' or perhaps 'you're not important enough for me to respond to and I'm too busy anyway'. Any of these could be correct, but we have no way of knowing which one. We start to resent the person for not responding and a natural reaction then is to start behaving in the same way and not respond to their messages promptly. This quickly creates a culture of bad corporate manners.

Good leaders, good communicators

The best leaders inspire their teams through clear communication, and the best organizations promote brand alignment, as well as respect and accountability with clear communication. In business leadership, I'm a great believer in, 'communication, communication, communication'. It makes no difference whether it's business, sport or politics; the best leaders are those who are the best communicators in all forms. They have strong values and are transparent with those values. Their teams look up to them and are inspired by them. If you want to achieve the maximum buy-in to your corporate brand then you need to master your corporate communication.

Individuals in your teams want to feel pride in the company they work for and the leaders they work with and represent. Phil Jones, managing director of Brother UK Limited, has managed his personal brand well and made a name for himself as a speaker and thought-leader in the future of leadership. This has made him more visible in his role, inside and outside of the Brother UK business. He believes: 'We have entered an era of leadership where there is a shift from power to influence. By me speaking and attending events I have the opportunity to communicate the brand of Brother UK so much more.' This of course also communicates strong and clear messages to his employees and gives them a sense of pride in their CEO.

In summary, we have looked at the various ways in which your brand can be strongly represented by methods and means that are not necessarily the obvious ones. As we move into an era that is focused on the total customer experience and how a company makes us feel as consumers and suppliers, or indeed employees, I would recommend putting together a specific plan of action to assess these areas of your business. This should look at how you might be leaking brand investment, as well as the opportunities to make a significant difference to the impact your brand has on all your stakeholders. In Chapter 3, I will be looking specifically at how you make your employees feel about you as a company and how we can tighten and heighten employee and the employer brand with personal branding in mind.

References

MarketingCharts (2013) [accessed 8 October 2015] 'Bad customer service interactions more likely to be shared than good ones', MarketingCharts, 15 April. Available from: www.marketingcharts.com/online/bad-customer-service-interactions-more-likely-to-be-shared-than-good-ones-28628/

Simpson, S (2015) [accessed 8 October 2015] 'UGRs: the way we *really* do things around here' UGRs. Available from: www.ugrs.net/index.php?section=92 – (2015) [accessed 8 October 2015] 'More about UGRs' UGRs. Available from: www.ugrs.net/more-about-ugrs

Employee brand and employer brand

03

Employee brand and employer brand are often confused and/or considered to mean similar things – in reality they are quite different. However, they both come down to the one core element that will project a strong employer brand or a strong employee brand more than anything else – people behaviours. Therefore, they are heavily interlinked and are dependent on each other.

Peter Cheese, CEO of the Chartered Institute of Personnel and Development (CIPD) in the United Kingdom, told me, 'Employer Brand and Corporate Brand are the flip sides of the same coin. Employees then need to live that brand consistently. Achieving this alignment may require a significant shift in behaviours.'

In this chapter we'll be focusing on how you take both employee brand and employer brand to the next level of engagement throughout your organization. This is not about creating your employer brand strategy (you probably have one in some form in place already); however, it may give you some ideas on how to expand yours to reach more effective levels and results. We will focus more on how you maximize the impact of that strategy by strengthening how the employee brand is implemented and realized throughout the company. We'll look at:

- the differences and correlations between employer brand and employee brand;
- the missing elements that make the real difference;
- how you can assess the level of engagement with your corporate brand among your employees;
- ways to improve engagement and effect the changes you need for competitive advantage;

- attracting and retaining Generations Y and Z;
- team branding for deeper engagement.

Making the distinction

In the simplest of definitions here's how we could describe employer and employee brand:

- employer brand – your company's reputation as an employer;
- employee brand – the process by which employees internalize and then project the corporate brand and reputation.

They are intrinsically linked because both are projected most powerfully by your people. This is impacted by how they feel about your organization and subsequently how they therefore behave. As a result of this emotional response, employees project themselves and talk about the company in a particular way to the outside world. So the two are very much interlinked and are ultimately concentrated around people behaviours.

The employer brand is typically portrayed via the media (broadcast, print and social), and advertising and recruitment campaigns; however, this medium is now overshadowed by the human element and the reality of experience. How your leaders in particular project themselves is also becoming more and more central to the employer brand. New talents are influenced by what they hear from key people in an organization about the company and their personal brands too. They will ultimately choose the organization they work for based on the 'personality' of that company and this will come across strongly from its leaders. We'll be covering more on this in Chapter 4.

Within your company, you probably have some sort of focus on employer brand – a term that was first used in 1996 in the *Journal of Brand Management* by Simon Barrow and Tim Ambler (1996). This academic paper was the first published attempt to 'test the application of brand management techniques to human resource management'. You may even have an employer brand strategy. This term has been used widely since publication of the paper. However, I believe that deployment of such strategies within organizations frequently stops short of what is needed in order to fully address your corporate reputation today.

Employer Brand and Employee Brand are intrinsically linked via people behaviours

FIGURE 3.1 Interlinking of employee brand and employer brand

Recruitment impact on employer brand

Employer brand, as a source of strategic competitive advantage, has been the basis of discussion in recent years. In my experience it is often an area of great focus by large organizations today and as such is talked about frequently in in-house conferences and education programmes for employees. It is presented externally to all stakeholders at every opportunity. Companies seek to create the perception and sense of this being a great place to work in order to attract the best people, and the people who will be best aligned to the corporate brand and culture. They do this by using various recruitment and external HR practices that project the brand reputation of the company. It might be advertisements that show a certain type of person and working environment, or techniques in interviews that demonstrate the values, for example. If you want to attract top talent and hire the best and brightest employees, you need to understand that the best and brightest employees can work wherever they please.

I would imagine you have in place recruitment strategies that take into account finding the right people to support your brand, but how about a strategy or guidelines at least for the actual process for interviewing, personnel conduct during the interview, having the right people to interview and the follow-up communication? These are all representative of your employer brand to the candidates, and how they feel during the recruitment process will be a reflection in their minds of the culture of your company. This will get talked about. Are you sure you are managing and measuring this element of your employer brand effectively?

I frequently hear about negative interview experiences from contacts and clients. These experiences are always described from the angle of the people involved. In one recent example, from a 22-year-old graduate about an interview process with a large global finance organization, he told me he had felt less than valued because of the way he was communicated with post-interview. He had twice travelled for two hours for a series of interviews, but any form of communication in follow-up took four weeks, including a simple and courteous 'Thank you, we'll be in touch again shortly'. Understandably, by this time he had started to have doubts about working for the company. It did not feel good to him – was he going to be respected and valued by the people he had met and could potentially be working for?

Your employer brand can be damaged by doing absolutely nothing

---

At times, doing absolutely nothing can damage your employer brand and reputation as a company. Lack of communication is perceived very negatively by candidates and causes them to feel undervalued. This makes your employer brand vulnerable. Guidelines and training for your HR and recruitment teams should be in place to avoid the dilution of the brand in this and other ways. You may not remember every candidate that is interviewed, but they will remember you and how you made them feel. Perhaps treating your candidates the same way as you do a customer might not be a bad way to operate.

How recently have you looked at the careers page of your website? This tends to be added on to the main site and little attention paid to how it projects your employer brand. Arguably, a separate site is needed for careers so that the personality of the employer brand can be managed more powerfully.

Getting your employer branding right is critical in a business environment that needs to maximize investment and reduce costs. The cost of not getting the right people on-board in your business – people who will never be aligned to the culture you want to create or the values you have set – is significant. Not just in terms of replacing them, but also in the less tangible aspects of diluting the employer brand and creating an environment that loses you the right people, and potentially creating a negative experience for clients. Even though you try to contain comments on social media internally, leakages will happen and dilution of the employer brand occurs. Getting the right people on-board and engaging them in the corporate brand values to a level that makes them proud and committed to working for you reduces costs, but in addition it maintains corporate reputation to a level we can't easily measure.

According to a study from LinkedIn (LinkedIn, 2012), the stakes couldn't be higher. When top talent accepts a job offer, a strong employer brand is twice as important as a strong company brand, particularly for candidates under the age of 40. A strong employer brand reduces the cost of new hires by half and cuts employee turnover by 28 per cent on average. For employers seeking to increase productivity and cut costs, these findings indicate that establishing a powerful employer brand represents a sound business investment.

Getting the right people on-board and engaging them in the corporate values, drives cost-savings

FIGURE 3.2 The optimum employer brand

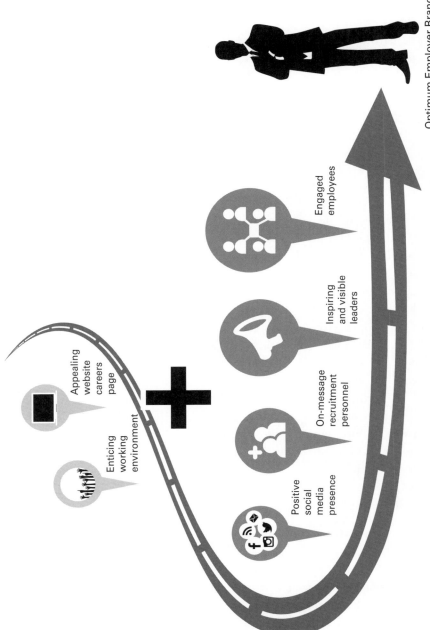

Appealing website careers page

Enticing working environment

Positive social media presence

On-message recruitment personnel

Inspiring and visible leaders

Engaged employees

Optimum Employer Brand

The working environment

In reality, the actual working environment can sometimes be far removed from the perception created, due to the behaviours of people. There is a significant height from which to fall when an employer brand is created but out of alignment with reality, and you may not easily be able to recover from this. Negative comments will spread quickly. It is simply good practice to project an accurate employer brand to the outside world and for employees to take ownership of the importance of their role in portraying it.

Every senior manager I've spoken to agrees that an internal culture will spill out to the outside world. It is simply not possible for a culture to be contained inside closed corporate doors only. For example, for years Google have had a great reputation for what they do and as a fabulous company to work for. However, social media often reports the opposite of Google as an employer. Whether it's accurate or not, as an outsider we really have no way of knowing, but the risk to Google's reputation as a result of these social media titters can spread, diluting the employer brand significantly. Google is no longer a start-up, it is a major corporation with all the challenges this encompasses. Perhaps therefore the image they always projected is not in alignment with present reality. It is crucial to present an accurate employer brand picture and then make sure every one of your employees lives up to it by believing in it themselves.

This is a statement made by the Dorchester Collection of Hotels: 'Our people are our most important asset. We are committed to treating every member of staff with dignity and respect, with processes that are fair and open.' This is a worthy statement to make and one that I suspect, from our work with them, is reinforced consistently by Dorchester staff. However, how many organizations make similar claims in the way they treat their staff and then pay no attention to monitoring this and to ensuring it actually happens to the degree they advertise? The gap between statement and reality is often significant.

We know that most employees leave their job because of their direct line manager. A bad line manager can take a good team of people and destroy it, causing the best employees to leave and the remainder to lose all motivation to stay. The way your managers behave is critical to your employer brand and it is very often overlooked because it's a challenge to deal with. However, these people will become 'weeds' in your teams and your company – they will create an undercurrent of bad behaviour which affects the overall culture in a team and the whole organization, that eventually eats up the good people and they leave. Too often this situation is ignored in the hope that it will improve, rather than addressed head-on, especially when the issue is with senior management.

While you need to find a way to eliminate the 'weeds' from your business, and it will of course take time if you allow it to happen through natural wastage alone, you can start to work on bringing about a culture in which the 'weeds' cannot thrive or survive. This is where employ*ee* brand comes in.

Employ*ee* brand is all about influencing the behaviour of employees to reinforce your corporate brand values in their everyday work. It is a strategy for creating behaviours that are 'on brand' and that reinforce the attributes that an organization wants to promote as part of its reputation or brand. The behaviours it seeks to create are both internal and external with the result that the corporate brand is strengthened with every communication. Sarah Dickins, executive people director of Friends Provident says: 'Keep it simple, be clear what your key messages are, and line everything up behind it – hiring, training, communication, reward systems, etc. Reinforce it at every opportunity as a leadership team.'

Simplicity seems to be a common theme among the companies getting the employee brand right, or that are at least on the right track. Peter Merrett, head of customer experience at JLL Australia, says: 'Our values are simple – making people's lives at work as easy and enjoyable as possible, is a key one for us. We believe it creates the right attitude of respect amongst the whole team.' He goes on to question, 'Trusting and empowering people is so easy to do so why don't all employers do this?' My view is that the mechanisms are not always in place at line management level in order for this to happen consistently, and often senior leadership and boards are not aware of this barrier.

In Chapter 1, we looked at the business model of the Swedish bank Handelsbanken. At Handelsbanken they have no formal employee or employer brand policy and see no need for one. They simply have a culture to help and respect each other. By keeping it simple, they believe they achieve a high level of understanding and engagement with the overall culture they want to create that also feeds through to the outside world.

When looking at the whole brand-to-people process in organizations, I spoke with Claire Harrison-Church, the marketing and brand director of Asda. I asked her how Asda ensure the people element of the brand works to improve brand messaging and ultimately increase return on investment of the marketing and brand budget. I also asked her how closely the marketing department works with the HR and learning and development teams to maximize the effect of brand awareness through training to create a strong employee brand. Claire said that they realize through recent metrics that brand recommendation is the most important piece to track. She added that, 'customer recommendations have the closest correlation to sales growth. If we can get our customers to love our brand, our business and our people, then they will talk about us positively and naturally shop more with us.' This reinforces my statement in the Introduction to this book, that 'the most important part of any corporate brand today is what your customers say about your brand to their contacts'.

As a result of these new findings and therefore the focus at Asda on what their customers say about them, they are now starting to work on socializing this through to their colleagues. Claire believes that 'because there is a very strong affinity between Asda colleagues and Asda customers, we know when we're doing a good job and a not so good job – by talking to our Asda colleagues'. The intention is for the advertising to help engage colleagues in the same way as it does with customers. This emotional engagement piece has been missing until now.

I personally wonder if this will be enough for individual colleagues to be able to interpret and internalize the brand as effectively as is needed in order to truly maximize brand investment. I put the question to Claire and her response was: 'We feel that Asda colleagues know the company well. The Asda brand *is* actually our Asda colleagues, more so than other retail brands.' Only time will tell how effective the advertising is in this respect. However, perhaps organizations in the retail world understand and achieve this with their advertising more than other sectors.

Claire finished by saying: 'The best advertising is, at the heart of it, expanding on the brand truth.' I would add that if the brand truth is the true experience we all have as clients and customers, then you have to be absolutely sure that what you are advertising truly replicates what your customers experience on a consistent basis.

I interviewed Jeremy Goring, CEO of the Goring Hotel in London. The Goring is the last remaining family-owned luxury hotel in London and is known for its royal guests, its impeccably English manners and its sense of wit and fun. I was intrigued to find out how they manage to maintain the consistency of service and their unique brand experience with every member of staff that guests encounter when they visit.

First, of course, they are a small hotel so managing their brand could be perceived as slightly easier than say a large multinational brand. However, this could go the other way too – because they are small there is more of an expectation for every element to be up to standard 100 per cent of the time. This is tough. However, as Jeremy Goring says, 'There is nowhere to hide in a small hotel – everybody has to be on the same page with the service and behaviours and maintain the standards, all the time.' In fact, this could apply to any small business.

Fun is top of the list when it comes to the reason they all work there and this they achieve incredibly well. In a subsequent interview with a range of employees there, fun and the feeling of a home-from-home for their guests were high on the list of reasons they love to work there.

In summarizing Jeremy Goring's key points on how they maintain the brand standards at The Goring with every member of staff, he said that they consistently:

- believe in what they are trying to achieve and are passionate about it;
- live the brand value of 'fun' every day in all they do;
- ensure employees are trusted to make the right decisions for guests;
- share positive guest feedback with all the staff to motivate;
- treat all employees as individuals and encourage them to use their initiative (they are not told how to answer the phone for example);
- make training less formulaic and more intelligent, with some twists.

Interestingly, when asking a selection of the staff about the brand of Jeremy Goring himself, the key words that consistently came through were: eccentric, fun, impeccable English, passionate, genuine. A pretty good match I would say, with the words he used himself to describe the uniqueness and success of the business!

Why we have to go deeper

I have found that many more companies state that an employer brand and/or an employee brand are key to success, than those who actually have a clear and structured plan for each. I frequently experience organizations who have a fabulous positive intention to engage their employees with their corporate brand values. They have their values displayed on walls all around their offices in the hope that employees will then live and breathe these values every day. However, it hardly ever works to the level they expect and need it to. Many times, I have had a group of senior managers in a training session and have asked them to give me their corporate values and vision and rarely can they give me them without a concentrated team effort! This tells me that they are not totally embedded in their hearts and minds. Internally, there can often be a focus on the values or words per se, rather than going further and getting to the heart of the individuals, and giving them the tools to interpret and project these values consistently in their own authentic way.

In Chapter 1, I referred to my interview with Andrew Murphy, retail director of John Lewis. John Lewis is a great example of a brand that has built a reputation that is consistently experienced by customers every single day. From the helpful, welcoming service, the attention to the personal details, the personality of the staff coming through and the handling of the 'never knowingly undersold' ethos they live by. We know what to expect and that expectation is met time after time. It is clear that the employee brand is managed closely. We've already heard some of the elements that make John Lewis a great company to work for; however, it is the emphasis on the role of the individual and how they are valued for what they personally bring that makes for a great employee brand there.

It's not just about customer service training

Employee branding programmes are often put in place to address the need for alignment between corporate values and people, and they tend to include customer service training and brand awareness. However, they rarely go to the level needed for individuals to really modify and realign their mindset and therefore their behaviours in the way they communicate.

Training that focuses more on the emotional intelligence of an individual, rather than the mechanics of how to do their job, will have a much greater impact on the effectiveness of changing of mindset and behaviours. The behaviours also become embedded for an individual at this level and start to become a habit and natural way of doing things. Internalizing the values of the organization and interpreting them in their own way, causes the employee to feel like they belong and that they are not trying to be somebody they are not. Feeling that they fit in to the culture is important to the way they ultimately behave.

If employees get to the level of feeling that they are doing something in alignment with their own purpose and values that truly motivates and drives them, then they will be more likely to behave authentically and feel like they are not just doing what is best for the company but for themselves too. This is the point at which you as an organization are truly engaging employees in the brand values and influencing them to behave in a way that supports those values.

The Asda way with people

CASE STUDY

Hayley Tatum, the senior vice president of people and stores at Asda (part of the WalMart Group), has had great success with employee engagement and I interviewed her to find what they are doing so well there. When Hayley arrived at Asda, she found that they were great at addressing the needs of their customers, but not so great at focusing similar attention on their 'colleagues' (employees). So she initiated and carried out, with the help of PricewaterhouseCoopers, the biggest piece of research they have done in 20 years, to find out what were the common trends and themes to colleague engagement across all parts of the business and at all levels.

The result of this research showed her that there were four key levers needed to ensure a high level of employee engagement:

- fairness – not meaning that everybody would be treated the same, but that everybody would be treated fairly;

- respect – having respect for each other, and colleagues wanted to be respected by their line managers in particular – they need to feel valued;

- opportunity – the chance to progress in their careers at their pace, if they choose to;

- pride – being able to feel a sense of pride in the company brand. They did not want to listen to bad news or feel embarrassed about their company.

These four levers have now become their pledges to all their colleagues and they guarantee that everybody will experience these consistently in their roles.

Of course, I was intrigued as to how they can guarantee this to over 7,000 colleagues, as we are really talking about creating a culture. Hayley believes this has been achieved for the following reasons:

- They send out an employee engagement survey every year, focusing on these four pledges, and this is sent from Hayley herself personally. It is introduced by a video from her that serves to provide a level of personality, commitment and care, rather than seeming faceless and being seen as just another anonymous survey that nobody will do anything with. Interestingly they get an incredible 92 per cent response rate with these surveys.

- They then act on the results – they form focus groups with colleagues from all levels and parts of the business, and share the results with them, check that they believe these are accurate and discuss what should be done. Colleagues therefore feel a real sense of contribution to the business and they help to shape the plan.

- Every quarter they do a 'pulse' survey with a random 10 per cent of colleagues, again from across the business. This allows them to keep an ongoing read on their performance where changes have been implemented.

They found that the most critical area with regard to the guarantee of the pledges rested with line managers. For all colleagues, the brand of the company *is* their line manager and how they behave. As Hayley says, 'We want all our colleagues to feel absolute pride in working for Asda and the people they work for'. This means ensuring that their local management and line managers all behave in a way that demonstrates respect to their teams and shows individuals they are valued. This is in addition to learning and adopting authentic leadership styles that are conducive to this environment.

Asda have an internal culture that truly supports their colleagues to be who they are and be the best they can be authentically. Our programmes at Asda had to be in total alignment with this. Our work there supported this ethos in providing leaders with the tools for being authentic and developing their own brand as well as recognizing the different personality types in their teams and what individuals need to feel valued and respected.

What works at Asda is the fact that their employee engagement is actually a very effective listening and follow-up action exercise. As Hayley says: 'We've got to keep listening, testing and following through with action.'

Brand training experience

As we've discussed, employee branding initiatives often fall short of the desired results, because they don't get to the hearts and minds of the individuals within the organization. To differentiate your brand from your competitors and drive customer loyalty, it is critical that you get to this level of engagement and most importantly provide them with tools that work and help them to internalize the brand messages so that they can deliver on these consistently. They will only do this if it is meaningful and authentic to them. In order to achieve this you need to give them an experience of what branding means in people terms, rather than the same old training programmes that fail to hit the mark.

Here are some key elements to consider when creating your brand training initiatives:

- Avoid providing only traditional and packaged customer-service training programmes.

- Consider what it is your customers need from their experience with your brand and focus your training programmes around that.

- Involve your client-facing staff in the design of the programmes – they are the ones who really know what is expected and appreciated by clients.

- Your training must address the 'what's in it for me' factor and get to the hearts and minds of the individual so that they fully understand how to project this brand experience with every interaction. Personal branding tools and techniques can achieve this – more on these techniques in Chapter 5.

- Ensure your managers are involved in the design and are supportive of the process and objectives. They are responsible for the success of the brand experience for customers in their stores, hotels, site locations and branches. Their leadership brand and style is critical to getting the results.

- Empower your employees (not necessarily just managers), to make intuitive decisions for clients and customers. Support them in this. I refer you back to the Langham Hotel ginger beer story in Chapter 2.

- Include ways in which to maintain momentum and keep focus. Introducing a reward scheme for delivering great brand experience should be considered.

CASE STUDY

We recently worked with the Grosvenor House, A JW Marriott hotel in London, to design and deliver a programme that was to improve the levels of employee engagement and guest satisfaction. Within Marriott Hotels, various training modules are delivered internally each year to align associates with the brand messaging and embed the strong value-set of their company. This works very well of course; however, the general manager felt that focusing on this area would benefit Grosvenor House, by getting to the absolute heart of the associate.

This would bring them to a level where they felt empowered to be themselves along with a deep understanding and appreciation of the prestigious hotel that they work for. The intention was that they should understand their personal brand, and then what they specifically bring to the overall service experience for the guest.

In order to achieve this, we first needed to gain buy-in of the executive team. We worked with them as a group and then individually, in order to immerse them in the personal branding process, so they could connect with the power of the training first-hand. This way it would filter down to associates more effectively. We needed to gain absolute clarity of the Grosvenor House brand to start with. We then drilled down to each team member's personal brands, using feedback and tools to define the brand statements for each. We then worked on ways in which they could project their brands authentically, build visibility and profile and effectively communicate with their teams in a way that was in alignment with their natural style, but also in a manner that reinforced the hotel brand.

Over a period of five months every single member of staff (of over 500) attended a Walking TALL session, covering the Grosvenor House unique brand, on a level that they could connect with, and that meant something to them. However, most importantly we were able to make them feel that they each contributed something exceptional by tapping into their value set and their personal brand, and giving them tools to project this every day, with every communication they had internally and with guests.

The results were incredibly positive. Grosvenor House's employee engagement survey reported an increase of 5 per cent in the first year and a further 2 per cent in the following year. In addition, they reported an unprecedented 15.9 per cent increase in staff behaviours in their measurement of being 'warm and hospitable to guests'. Guest satisfaction overall increased from 78 per cent to 80 per cent. This was attributed to the programmes that we implemented. General manager Stuart Bowery added that the initiative most importantly 'gave each individual employee the tools and inspiration to take their personal brand into their own hands, strengthen it and deliver a better experience for our guests as a result'. It is when we get to this level of engagement that behaviours start to change.

The task after any training programme or engagement initiative is to keep the momentum going, not just for existing staff but also for new people joining the organization. For Grosvenor House, we have provided them with a licence for their trainers to deliver the Walking TALL principles in-house whenever needed, to keep the messages alive and at the forefront of their everyday work, at all levels. When you're next in London, go and experience it yourself!

Another reason that the desired level of engagement is sometimes not achieved is that there is too great a degree of distance between the executive level where the brand values have been established, often along with a brand agency, and the individual person attempting to project these. Bringing it down to a team level, by creating a team brand can aid this process and gain greater results, as it becomes more localized and meaningful to the individual. We will cover more about team branding later in the chapter.

Many companies will say that their success is down to their employees, but a much smaller number actually put in the required effort and investment relative to the stated importance of their people. Southwest Airlines do it very well and use it to gain competitive advantage.

At Southwest Airlines they appear to get three major things right, in particular with their employee branding. First, they recruit the right people who have 'fun' in their DNA. Then they remain true to their value of *people* being at the very heart of what they do, whether that's their 46,000+ employees or their customers; and then because of how they do things they have their customers singing their praises too. Their employees are involved in their branding decisions and feel valued as a result. We often hear stories of how Southwest and their employees have gone the 'extra mile' to help customers and as a consequence they have become known for their extraordinary customer service.

Overplaying it

Care has to be taken not to over-engineer employee brand initiatives. Of course, it makes sense to have behaviour guidelines in customer service for example, but 'over-scripting' in terms of customer interaction can lead to a sense of falseness and an unauthentic brand image being projected. Remember, for example, the famous 'Have a nice day' statement that all McDonald's employees were told to say at the end of every transaction. Not only did it not work well in the United Kingdom and perhaps other countries outside of North America, it was rarely delivered from the heart of the individual, was meaningless and quite possibly had a negative or laughable effect. Would it not have been better to give employees the guidelines to start and end the transaction on a high, positive note, but in their own individual way? This is where an attempt at employee branding can go badly wrong.

No company can hope to, or should plan to create employees that are 'moulded' from the corporate brand to the level that they lose their own self, their own creativity and authenticity. With Generation Y and Generation Z now coming through into the corporate world, this is certainly a dangerous path to go down. No organization should be seen to influence the behaviour of an individual in a way that is not congruent with that individual's brand. Hence the need to ensure you are recruiting the right people in the first place, with strong and accurate employer branding strategies and recruitment processes, but also that everybody is given the tools and guidelines to interpret the corporate values and reinforce them in their authentic way. Not only is this right and moral, it's significantly more effective from the employee and external stakeholder viewpoint.

Creative thought and innovation can also be hindered if an organization is not nurturing individual brands and encouraging them to be used. Companies today need individuality in their people in order to differentiate themselves against their competition. If some of the techniques in this book are implemented, this can be achieved in a structured way under the umbrella of the corporate brand. We'll be covering the specifics on personal branding in Chapter 5.

CASE STUDY

Several years ago I was working as a consultant and coach with a large accountancy firm on their partner track, high-performance programme. I was invited to sit in on and observe several masterclass sessions where the delegates were asked to debate and discuss a specific topic, present individually and in groups, and manage one-to-one client meetings. I then had to produce a report on each person covering their impact, their brand image and executive presence and then coach them all individually. Not long into the coaching programme, I began to realize that they had received so much feedback and training as part of this talent programme that they had 'lost' themselves and consequently were trying to be somebody they were not. They just didn't know how to manage the feedback effectively as nobody had coached them through this, and therefore they were going from one level of behaviour to the exact opposite to compensate. So, for example, an apparent need to play down confidence could result in an individual going to the other extreme and holding back in meetings, not speaking their mind and therefore not necessarily being their authentic self. The myriad of negative effects of this is obvious. Working with them all on a tailored, individual coaching programme that focused on their true authentic brand and how they wanted to be seen, created an almost audible sigh of relief that they could start to be who they really are and manage this in a consistent positive way. Managing the feedback they received in alignment with their brand gave them a clearer personal development plan that made sense and gave the company what they actually wanted from their high performers.

The lesson here is to examine how exactly you are deploying your employee brand strategy – or even *if* you are – and whether it is giving your employees what they really need in order to live the corporate values in their own way. Are you potentially giving too much feedback to individuals in your talent programmes for example, and not enough know-how and tools to manage the feedback effectively? In which case, you could risk losing valuable personality and authenticity in your brand. If not, you are in danger of diluting your brand investment and at worst losing valuable talent from your organization. This will only become even more of a challenge in the future with Generation Y and Z filtering through into your organization – more on this later on in this chapter.

What makes a company great to work for?

When I analysed the list for the Top Fortune 100 companies to work for it was clear that there is a common thread as to why they reach the top. The survey for this list asks questions related to employees' attitudes about management's credibility, job satisfaction and camaraderie. They all rate very highly on these but there is a high focus among the top companies on the employees themselves and their wellbeing. Of course, we might say that's obvious. However, there are some specifics that go on in these companies that make a difference. For example at NetApp, the data storage company, vice chairman Tom Mendoza asks managers to notify him when they 'catch someone doing something right' and he then calls 10 to 20 employees a day to personally thank them. This culture of course spreads and gets talked about both internally and externally, enhancing both employee brand and employer brand.

Edward Jones Investment Firm, who maintain around 11,000 small offices throughout the United States, get 44 per cent of their new hires from employee referrals. This suggests there is a very strong employee brand here, where employees trust their company and its leaders enough to refer their contacts and friends.

Another thread with these top companies to work for is that they seem to have a high degree of social responsibility. At the Boston Consulting Group, the elite management consulting firm, employees receive $10,000 to volunteer at a non-profit organization for example. Other companies I spoke to recognize the need to raise their game when it comes to being socially responsible, as they know it has an impact on how effectively they attract talent from Generation Y and Generation Z in particular. Phil Jones, managing director of Brother UK Limited, believes that his time spent as a public speaker on stage at industry and academic events serves to create a public awareness of the employer brand of Brother UK. It informs others first-hand of the culture and social purpose of the company, such that no PR campaign can achieve to the same levels.

Measuring your current position

While this chapter is not about creating your employer or employee brand strategies, you may find these five key principles from Phil Owers useful in forming a basis if you don't have one. Phil has spent 17 years working with the world's best-known global brands to help them attract and retain the best talent.

1 *Employee value proposition* (EVP): Research and measure what your current employees and management consider to be the reasons they joined your organization and why they continue to work there. Use the EVPs to effectively communicate to potential and current employees what your values are and what it's truly like to work for your organization. Ensure you connect with your target audience and attach value to what they can achieve, such as investment in their future or the opportunity to make a real difference.

2 *Brand power*: What makes you stand out from your competition; does your brand provoke an emotional response? How effectively are your key messages being communicated? Focus particularly on what makes you different, why you stand out. It's the differences that attract top talent, the sense that they will be involved with something rare or even unique.

3 *Brand experience*: With the edges between employer brand and corporate brand becoming increasingly blurred, it's vital that both

your employer brand and corporate brand deliver on their promises; there is no hiding place from negative press, and what affects the brand will damage the employer brand and vice versa. It is imperative that potential employees can see a clear link between your brand and the experiences of your current employees.

4 *Brand appeal*: Is your brand image reflective of how your organization sees itself? For example, if you consider yourself to be a modern and forward-thinking organization, does your corporate 'look' support this or is it looking dated? Does your brand carry credibility? There are great examples of brand image projecting strongly onto employer brand – Apple, Google, Virgin – but I'm sure you can immediately think of brands where the opposite is true.

5 *Brand activation*: Is your brand being accurately deployed across all your campaigns consistently and effectively by all your stakeholders, through all your channels in every single country? If the answer is no, then you risk undoing all the investment of time and money spent building your brand. Very few organizations measure and control this effectively.

By using these five key principles as the basis for your employer brand strategy, by focusing on the retention of your current talent, then adding in all of the other bells and whistles that attract the attention of future talent, you'll quickly gain competitive advantage.

Assessing how your employees feel about the brand

The real drivers behind employee behaviours, therefore your employee brand and ultimately the employer brand that is projected, are the feelings they have about working for you and your brand, and how they are treated. Therefore, you clearly need to understand what the current situation is in this respect.

There are various ways to do this. However, in my experience long questionnaires get low response rates, whereas a few simple questions might not only give you a better response, but more valuable information too. Remember that employees want to give you feedback – just make it easy for them.

A valuable tool for measuring current employee engagement with your brand is Customer Thermometer (**www.customerthermometer.com**). It was originally developed for measuring customer satisfaction and still is used this way. However, it has been proven to provide a strong response rate for gauging employee engagement. The data as such is of course incredibly useful for highlighting areas that need attention in order to enhance employee brand. There is a place for traditional annual employee engagement surveys of course; however, we find that Customer Thermometer provides some hugely valuable data on how your employees are feeling right now about working for you. You need to regularly sense the staff 'heartbeat' as Lindsay Willott, the creator of Customer Thermometer says: 'By using a monthly solution, you can vary the survey questions you ask. Some months you could ask about working environment, other months you could ask about satisfaction with workload or stress. Doing it for one month won't work. You need to see trends – you need to show you are serious as a company about the process and so repeating monthly would be the key to success.'

The system they use is mobile too, so it's easy for employees to answer the question. It uses a simple one-click traffic light system of red, amber, green and each response is tracked back to the individual, so any issues are immediately highlighted. Busy employees are more likely to complete something this quick and simple and they feel connected and valued for their responses.

Some examples of simple questions you can ask each month:

- How are we doing for you as a company?
- Do you recommend our services and products?
- Are you proud to work here?
- How is your direct line manager doing for you?
- Are we a fair and ethical company?
- Do you feel valued?

Having gathered this data over a period of a few months you will start to get a good feel as to whether your employer brand is being represented well by your employees and how they are feeling. If not, the gaps should start to become clear for you to address.

Generation Y and Z considerations

A particular consideration when it comes to how effective your employer brand is has to be the emergence into the corporate workplace of Generation Y, sometimes called Millennials. Generation Y are generally considered to be those born between the early 1980s and 2000s. Following them, is Generation Z, born since 2000, sometimes referred to as the Digital Generation. By 2020, Millennials will represent half of our leadership positions. Therefore, investing in creating an employer brand that appeals to them, is not investing in the long term, it's critical investment required now for the near term.

Both Generation Y and Z create a whole new level of focus for employee and brand engagement that quite possibly many organizations are not yet ready and prepared for. These people represent the talent and leaders of the future, and they demand a different set of working life criteria than Generation X and Baby Boomers before them. We effectively have four levels of generation in the workplace now, so as well as having a diverse set of employee brand challenges, we cannot just rely on previous techniques, processes and initiatives to attract and retain these people. You have to look at what is required today to achieve and perhaps maintain employee engagement and an attractive employer brand with this generation in mind. Some of the key areas that are generally more important to Generation Y and Z than previous generations are:

- recognition;
- fast career progression;
- variety of work;
- transparent and authentic leadership;
- great leadership reputation;
- empowerment;
- respect among peers;
- social responsibility;
- less internal politics;
- pride in their company.

Of course, these are not applicable just to Generation Y and Z. Some apply to Generation X and Baby Boomers too. However, the next generation will be more demanding of these if they are to join you and stay with you.

Brown Brothers Harriman is a global financial services firm, headquartered in the United States. I spoke to Tim Cote, VP of service delivery at their Poland office in Krakow, about how they attract and retain Generation Y. They have been incredibly successful there in bringing on-board and retaining a large proportion of graduates. In fact graduates account for 68 per cent of the entire Brown Brothers Harriman Krakow workforce. Tim told me that they have focused on two key areas:

- supporting internal mobility and offering different career paths within the Bank;
- recognition and credentialing.

He says: 'We have a recruitment model based around development and retention, not attrition. We put significant effort into supporting this model.'

Brown Brothers Harriman know they have to consistently seek to keep on top of this if they are to remain an employer of choice. They are able to offer graduates the opportunity to explore different careers across multiple business lines. For example, it's not unusual for a graduate to start off as an operations analyst, then to move into client service a few years later, and into project management after that. They offer and encourage mobility throughout their teams, with the result of creating well-rounded executives for the future.

They have also been proactive in addressing the need for constant recognition and faster career progression. Generation Y will expect to be promoted after 12 months in their initial role, whereas previous generations might expect to be two to three years in their role before being considered for promotion. At Brown Brothers Harriman, they have adopted a specific credentialing process throughout the first few years of an employee's career. Through formal training certifications in conjunction with promotions that recognize technical mastery of their roles, this generation of talent receives the required respect and sense of progression that they crave.

Generation Y in particular need to know how what they do affects the company as a whole and to understand their work's higher purpose. Involve them where you can in discussion forums, company events and perhaps environmental causes you may be involved in as a company. They are the most humanitarian generation we have in the workplace right now.

Great employer brands for Millennials

In 2015, Fortune and Great Place to Work published their first-ever ranking of the best workplaces for millennial workers – a list of 100 employers who scored the highest among workers under the age of 35. The Millennial respondents to the survey say they most desire open communication, risk-taking, collaboration, support among employees and few internal politics.

Clearly a high degree of change needs to happen within a large percentage of organizations in order to meet the demands of the incoming generations.

Some questions you can ask yourselves as an organization that will assist in achieving a workplace attractive to Generation Y are:

- Do we have a recognition programme that is visible, meaningful and motivating?
- Do our recognition programmes provide the opportunity for Millennials to compare their performance to others?
- Do we give our Millennials high-profile opportunities to increase their visibility?
- Do we give our Millennials the opportunity to work outside of their immediate team?

Reverse mentoring

As a leader in your organization, a good insight into the hearts and minds of Generation Y is clearly critical. I've seen great results from leaders adopting a reverse mentoring technique for themselves. This basically involves taking on a Generation Y mentor and as a result understanding the business from the viewpoint of fresh eyes and minds that come from an alternative angle and with instant technology links to our future. Try it and make it part of your development plan as a leader.

The Generation Y TV ad

If you were to create a TV advertisement for Generation Y and Z as your employees of the future, what would you put in it and what would it look like? This will really help to shape the thinking behind what your employer brand should look like and portray to your target market right now and for the coming years. This might be a worthwhile exercise for your leadership team at the next team meeting.

Whose responsibility is it anyway?

An area for concern that I have for companies is that often you are not clear about who is responsible for employer branding. When conducting my research, it was often difficult to get to the appropriate person. This was slightly less so for employee branding as it's really about people development, therefore clearly an issue for HR or learning and development. Within companies, some people believe HR is primarily accountable for employer branding, and others view marketing and/or corporate communications as being principally responsible. It's not difficult to imagine what would happen if key leaders in your business couldn't agree about who owns finance, or marketing or IT. One of the most important functions in your organization for its future success is attracting the people who will lead it into the next stages of development. Surely therefore you need a crystal clear function lead, that is also clear throughout the business?

Team branding

Have you ever considered that there might be a very wide gap between the corporate intention of the values, mission statement and vision, and the actual interpretation and internalization of these messages by the people who you need to project them every day? All that great work you carried out as an executive team, together with the expensive brand agency you used to create these innovative and meaningful messages may not be getting through in the way you thought they would and you need them to. This is simply because the intense affinity you've had with the values, for so long in their creation at top level, is not replicated with the same intensity lower down the organization. The energy around them is diluted as it filters down.

Bringing the brand to a team level can be an effective way of localizing the messaging to make it more meaningful across your employee base.

FIGURE 3.3 Closing the brand gap

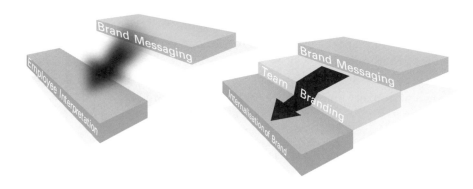

Cascading the corporate values down to team level, and allowing department managers to create with their teams, a set of values, a vision and a brand for their specific team, is a highly effective way to ensure that messaging is robust, relevant and sustainable throughout the organization.

When we roll out our personality of the brand programmes within organizations, our approach is to work with team groups wherever possible. This has the double benefit of making your values clear at a much more local level and also giving a much-needed brand to a team. Managers tell us that:

- there is a lack of clarity on what their team actually does in other parts of the organization;
- the team is not as appreciated as it should be;
- we have a lack of engagement within the team;
- team members don't really know what other team members do;
- we want to be better positioned as a team and really known for what we do.

By addressing the team brand challenge individuals can feel more involved in the specific goals and vision of the team (which of course will contribute to the overall corporate objective), and clearly see how their work has real impact. In Chapter 5, we look at how to establish what you *really* do – this process can have an incredibly positive effect on individuals in a team, as they come to fully appreciate how their personal contribution matters and understand the change that happens as a result.

In Chapter 1, I mentioned Handelsbanken and their highly successful business model of localization. At Handelsbanken they believe that if you give the power to the local branch, then the best decisions for the customer are made. The staff there have a deep appreciation of what the branch is trying to achieve as a team, as well as the customer's specific needs. We could apply this same philosophy to the teams within your organization – if every team member were to understand the vision and values of the team, and be directly involved in creating them, they can more easily make sense of them in all their roles and interactions and reinforce them every day. They will become proud to live the values. The team brand messaging should reflect the overall ethos of the corporate brand, and become an offshoot, taking on its own personality and relevance for the team objectives.

Team brands become offshoots of the corporate brand

Involve the team

At commercial property real estate company, JLL Australia, they work hard on creating an extraordinary customer experience. Head of customer experience, Peter Merrett told me that they involved a huge number of people across the business when it came to deciding what the values should be. So they got a high degree of buy-in, as all departments contributed. He said, 'They shared the pride and the passion because they were part of the process.' It sounds simple really doesn't it, but it's not common practice in my experience to involve people across the business.

In fact, they use a large amount of innovation at JLL Australia to create consistent positive touch-points to improve the customer experience. A common thread I can see is that they value, respect and involve people as much as possible. For example, because of the nature of their business they outsource in several areas, so they recognize they could have a challenge with lack of consistency of values expression via contractors. Therefore, they fully involve their contractors, including plumbers, cleaners and engineers in their customer service training and monthly social get-togethers. They then feel part of the team, and they share and reinforce the value set.

Earlier in this chapter, I described the programme delivered for the Grosvenor House Hotel. Even two years later, the doormen, front of house associates and restaurant staff still talk about the principles we covered in their training and tell me about everyday occurrences where they've been able to use them. They felt as important as the management team when going through the training programme and are now able to appreciate their pivotal role in the general manager's overall objectives. This was due to the localization relevance we were able to bring to them in the programme, using specific examples that they could relate to. It also helped that Stuart Bowery, the general manager personally introduced every training session we had. As a result, the principles have become deeply embedded in their daily lives.

The effect of not involving the team

I recently experienced how things can go badly wrong when you embark on a major project or initiative that requires total buy-in across the organization for it to receive the support it needs to be successful. In this particular example, excitement was building at the annual convention of an association of which I was a member. Nobody really knew what the announcement was, although of course the usual rumours were circulating as with anything of this ilk. There was a huge build-up to the announcement on stage and when the 'big thing' turned out to be a re-brand and name change, there was a weak ripple of applause for the new name that quickly died away. What followed in the days and weeks to come was a significant rejection and rebuke by members that resulted in a reversal back to the old name within a matter of weeks. The clear lesson learned was that when you need to effect a change that you expect all your employees to embrace and reinforce, involve them (or representatives at team level) at every step of the way. When you need your team to reinforce the messages that are at the core of your team's brand, you need their buy-in and active contribution. Team branding can achieve this.

Part of the big picture

The story goes that during a visit to the NASA Space Center in 1962, President John F Kennedy noticed a janitor sweeping the floor. He inter-rupted the tour and walking over to the man said, 'Hi, I'm Jack Kennedy. What is your role here?' The janitor answered, 'I'm helping to put a man on the moon'.

Whether the story is actually true or not, or if it's evolved over time, it's easy to see how we can more effectively engage every person in the overall objectives for the business if they are clear about the specific role they play and their part in the overall company objective. They also need to be valued for their contribution and the most junior member of your team needs to understand the vision in order for it to be successful. The 2003 England rugby team coach, Sir Clive Woodward, was famous for inspiring every member of the team, whether the fly half or the team coach driver, to be the very best in the world at the job they did. When your entire team embraces this type of attitude, amazing things will happen for employee engagement.

The process of team branding

I would suggest a good starting point might be to take a look at your executive team. How coherent are you? How are you perceived as a team internally?

CASE STUDY

I was asked by a head of learning and development in the technology sector, to work with the executive team on clarifying the brand of the team, and then to help them to project a consistent and coherent message to the company. When I worked with them it was clear that they each had differing views of what the leadership team stood for and how it should be projected. They even had inconsistent views as to what the corporate brand was. All six of them were geographically dispersed, were from different cultures and therefore seemingly had quite diverse views of how this team should be perceived. This was having a detrimental effect on how effective the team was regarded as being by the rest of the company and in particular their direct reports and the management teams below them. It was affecting the confidence the company had in the leadership team too.

There was an unspoken resistance to addressing this imbalance or even to recognize its existence, with the exception of the managing director. In addition, there was a lack of clarity on who officially reported to who and where, and as a result they were all battling for their personality to shine through and for their position to be visible and heard. I had a real challenge on my hands.

I first of all worked on the executive team brand messaging. Because of the cultural and personality-type differences in the team, I had lots of 'enthusiastic' discussion about what various words actually mean.

I then moved to looking at their personal brands and how they individually reinforce and reflect the team brand and most importantly, the corporate brand. This is when the connection truly started to take shape and we all began to get somewhere. They had never really thought about their personal brands before and now they were starting to understand and appreciate the huge effect their brands have on the corporate brand as a whole. This added a level of clarity not only to their own brand, but also to each other's brands, and what they each brought to the table. This had the effect of diluting the previous distracting challenges of 'muscling' for the top voice.

Eight months on, we had an executive leadership team that were really clear about the brand of the team (under the overall messaging of the company), and individually had a new-found confidence and clarity in their own personal brand that enabled them to lead and present in a way that truly engaged their teams and the wider employee base. Quite simply, they started to be real and 'human' in the eyes of their people. This has played out in the way they interact with people generally, how they value the managers that report direct to them and the way in which they present publicly at corporate conferences.

What can you achieve with team branding?

Start with working out what is most important to you to achieve with this process:

- To build a clear and compelling team brand, with your vision and mission, created with the input of all the team members – or at least a diverse selection of individuals if the team is large. You can consider splitting the team into sub-sections if this is appropriate.

- To improve the perception of your team internally and externally.

- To create a series of sound bites that each team member is comfortable with and that convey the core values and purpose of the team. The purpose should relate to and perhaps be a sub-set of the overall corporate mission.

- To create a team brand statement that encompasses your values and unique purpose as a team.

- To create better internal and possibly external promotion for the team, online and face to face.

- To create a better understanding of individuals' skills and personalities within the team.

- To enhance the congruence between the team messages and individual behaviours.

- To build our credibility and effectiveness.

So how do we do it?

Remember, much the same as your personal brand, your team has a brand whether you have worked on it already or not. You need to gain some input into what the current perceptions are before you start. The current brand you have is portrayed by how your team collectively behaves and how others experience it. Ask the following questions:

1 **What are the current perceptions of us as a team, internally and externally?**
Gather feedback from various parts of the business, from people at different management levels and diverse levels of interactions with your team. Highlight where the biggest areas of confusion and weakness are that need to be addressed.

2 What does our team consistently do?
What are the common behaviours that you project that may be subconscious? Look at the positives and negatives.

3 What do we do really well, and not so well? What do we need to be better at and what do less of?
Make sure you spend time separately on the positives and the negatives. We can't be addressing the negatives and be creative at the same time as we use different parts of the brain for each.

4 Who are our clients?
Which audiences do you serve? What do each of them need from us?

5 What are the key values we stand for?
What is most important to us as a team? What do we always strive for in terms of excellence at what we do?

6 How do we each interpret those values?
How do each of you see those values manifesting themselves in your everyday communications and work?

7 What collective impression do we leave on our clients?
Ask your clients this – what do you get when you work with us? What are we known for most of all?

8 What do we want to be known for most of all?
This may equate to your vision statement. You need to be crystal clear about this.

9 What are we brilliant at?

It's easier to be great at the things you are passionate about. What does the team exist for and why did you join it in the first place?

Have each member of the team do some thinking and reflection on these questions on their own, coming up with their own views first, and then bring all the input together for discussion.

You will need to achieve a defined set of behaviours that the team have come up with and are consistent with, that are filtered from and encompass the ideas you collect. If the team have been involved in creating these behaviours, they are much more likely to demonstrate them consistently, and provide feedback to others if things start to lapse. They all have a personal buy-in to what has been created.

What does a team brand statement look like?

As a result of the above exercise, you will need to create a team brand statement so that everybody is clear about what you stand for and provide to the business.

There are no real rules for a team brand statement – it's what you feel as a team clearly depicts who you are and how you want to be perceived. Here's an example framework that may help you get started:

Example team brand statement for a corporate communications team:

We're very proud to be known as the central glue that holds all lines of communications in the business together. Because of our ability to understand all the principle brand messages for the company, and the key players who can deliver those messages to the media effectively, we are the team to go to in times of crisis or celebration, or in seeking an opportunity for extra exposure for an individual or the business as a whole.

We are creative and collaborative in our approach, and we are able to see the helicopter view of the business, enabling us to clearly get to the pertinent opportunities to express our brand to the outside world.

We have fun, we have endless energy and we love to connect people. We do this with the utmost professionalism and integrity and strive to always provide the very best global exposure there is for our people and the business.

Don't leave your team brands to chance – you will miss a huge opportunity to step up and shine in the organization personally and as a team as a result. Empower your line managers to engage in this process and remember a team brand is not just for show and image, it's about being more effective, productive and credible. Now build a plan to get started.

In summary, whatever way we look at brand – corporate brand, employer brand, employee brand, team brand – it all comes down to people behaviours and consistency, and all are interlinked and drive each other.

The way you treat your people will show up somewhere, so never has there been a more crucial time to activate plans to provide your most valuable asset – your people – with the tools to be the best they can be for themselves and your brand.

To attract the talent you need, you have to have an employer brand and reputation that is trustworthy, unique, authentic and consistent. This begins with having a disciplined approach with clear objectives and strategy and above all clear ownership throughout the company.

References

Barrow, S and Ambler, T (1996) The employer brand, *The Journal of Brand Management*, **4**, pp 185–206 (October)
LinkedIn (2012) 'Why your employer brand matters' LinkedIn for Business. Available from: https://business.linkedin.com/content/dam/business/talent-solutions/regional/nl_nl/campaigns/PDFs/why-your-employer-brand-matters-whitepaper.pdf

Leadership 'off-brand' behaviours

04

There is no doubt that your leadership team are responsible for and represent one of the most powerful influences on your corporate brand and reputation today, over and above all other aspects. Their style and behaviours are a catalyst for the employee brand you create due to the standards they set, the employer brand that is projected, and the culture ultimately maintained. This is a responsibility that merits a high and constant level of assessment, measurement and adjustment. We are in a business world where this simply has to be at the very core of your brand strategy if you are to compete effectively and achieve the goals you set yourselves as an organization.

We are going to focus in this chapter on bringing leadership brand to the fore of your thinking and covering ways in which to address and adjust by looking at:

- how the culture is influenced by leadership style and behaviours;
- top-down and bottom-up cultures;
- CEO brand;
- the narcissistic leader;
- humour in the office;
- the effect line managers have on your brand;
- leadership brand and executive presence.

What is authentic leadership?

What your employees look for in your leaders today is a high degree of honesty, integrity and fairness and a feeling that they are genuine and not trying to be somebody they are not. Your customers are also looking for something similar. Authentic leadership means being aware of your strengths, limitations and emotions and behaving in a way that demonstrates this self-awareness. When leaders appear to put on 'an act' it will dramatically dilute the levels of trust their teams have in them and therefore their effectiveness in taking people with them. The follow-on effects of this are obvious.

In his book, *Authentic Leadership* (2004), Bill George, former CEO of Medtronic looked at what makes today's successful leaders successful. The thread that runs through the book is that they are first crystal clear about their values and what they stand for. Secondly, they are transparent with those values so others around them know what they stand for. They are therefore more effective at taking people with them and exerting influence. Thirdly, they don't compromise on those strong values. That is the toughest piece of course. Sometimes we are challenged on our values and have to do things that aren't necessarily in total alignment with our value set. However, we can probably live with it once or twice. If compromise is required regularly in our roles, then it's time to consider moving on.

You cannot lead productively today if your teams don't know who you are. They need a clear direction from a leader who is self-aware, genuine, is clear about what he stands for and is prepared to stand up for this. A level of vulnerability is also essential and this can only be achieved if you as a leader are totally comfortable with yourself.

I recently spoke in Europe at a conference for a large financial organization, focused on building confidence among their talent and female leadership in particular. In preparation for this event I was part of a planning forum to discuss the objectives and other elements of the conference. One session was to be a panel of senior-level leaders who were to share how they had got to where they are now and the mistakes and challenges along the way. The two questions they struggled with most were: 'Can you tell us about a time when you misjudged a situation and made a wrong decision, and how you recovered?'; and 'Tell us about a situation where you felt out of your comfort zone in terms of your abilities to achieve success.' Of course, both of these were asking them to expose their vulnerability with the result of showing the audience that it's ok to make mistakes because you can still get to where you want to be, and that as a senior leader you do not always get it right first time. They truly struggled with this exposure as they saw it, and in my view we never got to the true person behind the leader. Therefore the objective of the panel session, which was to help build confidence in their future leaders by showing that being out of your comfort zone is necessary to grow, was never met.

You cannot be authentic by trying to imitate someone else. You can learn from others' experiences, but you can't be successful if you are trying to be just like them. People trust you when you are genuine and authentic, not a replica of someone else. Former Amgen CEO Kevin Sharer, who worked as Jack Welch's assistant in the 1980s, saw the downside of this. 'Everyone wanted to be like Jack,' he said. 'Leadership has many voices. You need to be who you are, not try to emulate somebody else' (George, Sims, McLean and Mayer, 2007).

So the first step in great leadership is to establish who you are as a leader and how you want to be perceived, clarifying your own brand and value set. We will cover more on this in Chapter 5, Getting back on-message.

The CEO and corporate reputation

According to research by Burson-Marsteller in the United States, a CEO's reputation accounts for 50 per cent of a company's reputation (Jensen, 2014). In Germany, it counts for 63 per cent. Just like a product or service brand, a CEO's brand is a collection of powerful and clear ideas that people have of that brand. To be successful, the CEO needs to project a brand that is consistent with and in alignment with his or her value set. They need to be known for what they are great at and the uniqueness of their brand. It is this that will make them stand out and be successful – by being unique and different.

The CEO brand is not just an external face of the company – people see the CEO as a representative of the corporate brand on the outside but the face of the culture on the inside, thereby also impacting on the employer brand and the reputation of the company. The CEO brand can also very effectively inspire employees to do the best job they can for the company.

CEO brand impact

Whatever the personality of the CEO, we can be sure that it will have some level of impact on the brand perceptions of the company. This can be a good thing of course as what the CEO says and does can have as much impact on sales as TV advertising or marketing campaigns. Interestingly, according to the CEO Reputation Premium and Weber Shandwick's research, 50 per cent of executives say that their CEO's reputation impacted their decision to accept a position, and 58 per cent say it keeps them at their company (Weber Shandwick, 2015).

However, this can go badly wrong too – remember Tony Hayward of BP after the catastrophic oil spill and those famous words 'I want my life back'. He also previously stated that the amount of oil spilled into the Gulf of Mexico is 'relatively tiny' compared with the 'very big ocean'. The share price of BP slumped after this, as did his and BP's reputation. Mr Hayward's response also tainted the brand image of the whole industry so that huge efforts had to be applied to regaining their collective reputation.

On the other hand Richard Branson rarely makes public appearances, as he knows he's not great at it and not the best person to do it. However, after the Virgin Rail crash in 2007 he decided to speak to the press. Although the interview was hesitant and not slick, he came across as authentic and empathic saying the right things at the right times, without blame. This was yet another reinforcement of the strong Virgin brand via its chairman – worth more than any advertisement. Consumers can relate to him as the personification of the brand.

In a more recent example in 2015, the CEO of Merlin Entertainments, Nick Varney was interviewed after a serious accident involving one of their UK theme park roller coasters. In one particular instance, Mr Varney was interviewed by a TV presenter, after which a petition was signed demanding her sacking because of the harshness and persistency of her questioning. Mr Varney remained calm and composed yet empathic and professional. He gained much praise for his handling of this interview and as a result his brand has grown positively. He has become known for his professionalism and grace and, despite this being a tragic accident, the company has retained its dignity and brand, and its loss of share price is likely to recover fairly quickly.

There is often a misconception that brand management is in the hands of a company's communications and marketing team, particularly when a crisis happens. However, it's the CEO who holds the future of a brand in their hands. It is how they initially handle the situation personally in the face of the media that will recover the brand or not. It is also their opportunity to add a personal and human element to the brand that is much needed at these times.

How a leader responds to the challenge of taking responsibility can influence public feelings on a particular event. CEOs handling bad news ineffectively can have a detrimental impact on share price and reputation, and add to the list of damage already in place for a business. This happened recently when Peter Fankhauser, CEO of Thomas Cook, took too long to respond personally to the tragic incident of a family of two children who were killed by carbon monoxide poisoning in a Corfu hotel in 2006. He eventually apologized 'for all they have been through'. It was not the heartfelt response to such a tragedy that the public and the family involved quite reasonably had expected.

Whether we like it or not, the CEO brand projects what the company stands for, in the eyes of customers and shareholders. Business leaders are emerging from a period in which traditionally CEOs kept a low profile, except in times of crisis. This is rapidly changing and we're now in an era of social media and the ability for consumers to quickly spread a dilution of the corporate brand with comments about its leaders. We have also come to expect a rapid and human response.

In addition, employees can be inspired to do the best job by the brand the CEO projects. Feeling proud of the company you work for is a key element of employee engagement and feeling pride in senior management is a part of this. The CEO's brand adds the much-needed personality to the brand, in a way that no other means of marketing can do to the same extent. However, this brand needs to be defined, nurtured and exposed wherever possible and appropriate, and the brand story told – we will cover more on this in Chapters 5, 6 and 7.

Of course this goes further, it is the brand of the whole executive team that shapes the brand of the organization. This needs to be congruent with the values of the company and each personal brand within the team needs to dovetail with and be in synergy with the others. You also need to be cognizant of the need for the leadership team to complement the brand of the CEO, rather than contradict it. This is not to suggest, that all personal brands of the leadership team need to be the same or even similar, they just need to be in alignment and fully understood by each other, and consistently projected. In my experience, leadership team brands are often unclear, incoherent and nowhere near enough time and focus is applied to this aspect of corporate branding. Now is the time to address that.

If your employees are proud of, aspire to be like and talk positively about the leadership team this creates a powerful employee engagement element that is seen as critical in some organizations. Employees want to be proud of the leaders in their company when they see them interviewed on TV or quoted in a press article.

When it comes to training programmes to embed the values of the new brand throughout the organization, the leadership and executive teams can at times be deemed internally as exempt from needing this. Or perhaps they themselves see it as 'going through the motions', as they have of course been immersed in the re-brand process and there is the assumption that this training is 'just for their teams'. This is potentially a dangerous trap to fall into.

The executive team must not be exempt from brand behaviour training

Bottom-up or top-down culture

A culture cannot be created purely via a top-down approach. It has to be encouraged to emerge naturally from within an organization, and then reflected, supported and reinforced by the leadership team and senior management. Yes standards need to be set and inspiration provided from the leadership, however it will always be at the heart of the workforce that the culture is created and ultimately adjusted where necessary.

We could say that the culture of an organization is built from the bottom and shaped from the top. Or on occasions, tainted and diluted at and from the top. I have experienced many situations where a company is re-branding and wanting to embed the values and brand messages throughout the organization, but where I'm told from several angles that the leadership teams, or some individuals within the teams need to work on this too. It seems that at times, senior leaders are either lacking in self-awareness or deem themselves exempt from needing to modify behaviours in the way they expect their staff to. Executives are no different from everybody else – nobody admits to bad behaviours and everybody thinks they are better than the average. Similar to how most people think they are better than the average driver! So a good starting point is to acknowledge the fact that you may not be getting it right yourself all of the time and raise your level of self-awareness. Then you need to demonstrate that you are willing to admit that you can learn and improve by attending programmes yourself.

Feeling slightly uncomfortable? Could this be you?

Old style 'command and control' leadership has of course no place in today's corporate world. In any event, it was never effective in creating an environment or culture that was healthy for any company to maximize people effectiveness. It stifled creativity and innovation, and restricted individuals in being authentic in their behaviours. This was very much a top-down culture and today we need to recognize that the corporate behaviours and culture that exist in an organization are created from within, at the heart of the workforce. We need therefore to turn things on their head and look at them, not so much from a bottom-up approach, but from an organic growth from within the workforce that diffused throughout, all the way to the top, and down again. Of course the executive team and all senior leadership need to embrace and reflect the desired behaviours in all that they do internally and externally. Without this reinforcement, leakage will occur and result in confused and unclear employer brand messages, and ultimately the desired corporate brand message is not fortified.

The influence and impact of the leadership team

Your company, no doubt, has management development, talent and leadership training programmes and initiatives in place, or at least you are starting to create a framework for such a programme. In fact, with those of our clients who have a limited training budget, training is almost always concentrated at senior leadership or talent communities. You may also have induction programmes for new starters, and training courses for those aspiring to management positions of course. These may all have varying degrees of content and focus on your corporate values, what the organization stands for and what is expected of individuals. So let me ask you, what do you have in place for your executive leadership team that ensures that every one of you consistently reflects and reinforces the corporate values via your internal and external behaviours? What measures are in place for feedback on how you come across and what your personal brands stand for? My guess is that you, as a leadership team, neglect this area for yourselves and it's also an unwritten assumption that 'of course the leadership team represent the corporate values at all times – why wouldn't we?' In addition, how much do you encourage and allow, I mean *really* invite and allow, feedback for yourselves, and then act on it?

When I asked Sarah Dickins, executive people director at Friends Provident about how they ensure that the leadership are also 'on-message' with the brand messaging in their behaviours, she told me that in this last year alone they have spent £1 million on leadership training and this includes their board and their direct reports, amounting to 1,200 employees. 'Every member of the Executive Team has gone through this training. We've learned a lot about ourselves and each other by putting ourselves in challenging situations, and making ourselves a little vulnerable,' she says.

First, there is little time for you as a team to focus on this and secondly it's often considered a no-go area for heads of learning and development to question the behaviours of the leadership team, let alone provide a coaching or training programme that addresses this subject for them too. I am frequently told when developing personal branding programmes with learning and development managers, 'we're not sure yet how we're going to get the leadership team to take part in this too. They think the rest of the company need it but see themselves as exempt'. Of course, my reaction is, if you are really serious about getting the results and total buy-in to this programme then the leadership team have to take part. They not only need to be seen to embrace the concepts and live them, but quite possibly also really need the training and coaching themselves too. Is this the case in your organization?

Non-verbal leadership influence

It is often the non-verbal behaviours that have the greatest amount of influence on others. Generally, these are subconscious and present a lack of self-awareness.

A female board director I worked with, from a large global organization, was sent to me for coaching specifically because the way she presented herself was not congruent with the expectations of the company at that level. She was well-liked and professionally brilliant, however when she turned up at company events her interpretation of 'appropriate dress' was, I was told, not at the level expected by a board director. 'Leggings that were so old you could see through them, blouses that would often have a mark or stain on, and hair that needed a good brush through', were the descriptions used. This was truly getting in the way of her aspiration of becoming a non-executive director and in gaining extra exposure as an ambassador of the company. It was a very sensitive area to address as you can imagine. However, the point is, are you seeking the coaching and advice needed in this type of blind-spot area?

So having got this sensitive area on the table, let's look at what you could be doing to establish what's needed and then assess what has to be implemented. It makes sense that if you as a leadership team consistently represent and reinforce the corporate values authentically in the way you behave, then this will filter down to your management teams and thereafter their people, reinforcing the whole desired culture. As mentioned, the leadership team do not shape the culture, but they do infect and colour it with influential behaviours, creating a diluted and weakened culture, or if we get it right, a heightened and strengthened cultural environment that creates and encourages their teams to operate consistently and effectively in all that they do and to be the best they can be. The Water Tank Theory illustrates this:

FIGURE 4.1   The water tank theory

If you put a coloured dye in at the top of the tank of water, it will slowly but convincingly and permanently colour, taint or dilute the rest of the water in the tank. You simply cannot afford for this effect to happen with negative behaviours. In a positive sense, it will influence culture and behaviours throughout the organization, keeping them intact in a way that you need in order to stay competitive, stand out and remain relevant in your sector. You cannot hope to create the ultimate sustainable culture without paying close attention to the way you behave and therefore influence as a leadership team.

It is essential to role-model the behaviours you want to see in others throughout the company. For example:

- You want your teams to take control of their careers, personal development and attend training sessions? Then attend them yourself and be fully present (no sloping off early to go to urgent meetings or answer e-mails).

- You want people to turn up to meetings on time and fully prepared? Then do this yourself too with no exceptions.

- You advocate that you want people to get a better life balance? Then demonstrate this yourself by not being in the office all hours or answering e-mails in the middle of the night.

As soon as you stop exhibiting the behaviours you want to see in them, you give others the perfect excuse to stop too.

> Consistently emulate the behaviours you want to see in others

As Fred Astaire said, 'The hardest job kids face today is learning good manners without seeing any.' The same applies to leadership.

CASE STUDY

I was asked by an HR director to work with a CEO of a large finance organization in the United Kingdom, who needed help with the way he came across to employees and the media. I was told in the brief that people didn't really 'know' him; he never made time for anybody or spoke to employees in the office, and sat in his plush glass office on the top floor not really interacting at all unless he had to.

When I started working with him, I first of all discovered he was shy and introverted and also that he disliked interacting with people for the sake of it with no real agenda. I gathered some feedback from people from various levels in the company and yes, sure enough, they were feeling like they were invisible to him and that he had no interest in them as individuals. This was causing them to feel irrelevant and undervalued.

Of course we had to work on this as it was negatively affecting his brand internally and externally, and ultimately the brand of the company and how his employees felt about working there. It had a danger of leaking out too with potential negative effect on the business and employer brand.

Starting with his authentic brand, and how he wanted to be perceived, we worked on many areas of the way he communicated and represented his brand. Among other things, I suggested that instead of calling down from his office to the person he needed information from, he actually walk down there to see them, have a two-minute chat and request the information he needed. He liked this idea, as he said it had a purpose and it's not just small talk and wandering through the office for effect.

A few weeks later, however, I discovered that he had been going down to see the relevant person, but walking past many others to get there without even making eye contact. So it was back to the drawing board to address this too. We got there in the end and eventually people started to talk about him in a more positive way, without realizing that he had specifically worked on this aspect of his brand behaviours.

This alone was a huge lesson for my client. He realized that his brand was on show all the time and that people judged him, and to a degree the company, on how he projected himself.

At the end of the coaching programme, he stated that it had enabled him to put himself on a conscious track, and every decision he now makes and every communication he has is more in alignment with his brand and values and therefore those of the organization. In other words, he became more self-aware and more consistent in the projection of his personal brand because he'd found a way to be authentic and true to himself, as well as being more effective in the eyes of his team and wider employee base.

He said afterwards that a re-framing took place from which all his actions and behaviours could flow. As CEO he recognized that he demonstrated leadership behaviours in the choices he made, subconsciously, every minute of every day, whether they related to the way he presented himself, dealt with people or interacted with clients or employees.

The narcissistic leader

With the example above, the CEO was unaware of the impact he was having on the employees and ultimately on the internal culture, but was open to the feedback and able to embrace it and fix it. As a leader you need to have this level of self-awareness, the ability and willingness to listen to feedback and adjust behaviours where necessary, if you are to create and support a culture of trust, respect and transparency.

As we've seen earlier, the internal culture of an organization will spill out to the outside world at some point. This impacts employer brand and as a result the overall corporate brand. Narcissists have an exaggerated sense of their own self-importance, an increased need for others' admiration and a general lack of empathy. This is a common trait among CEOs to varying degrees, and in fact according to a research study by Illinois professor of psychology Emily Grijalva, the most effective leaders have a moderate level of narcissism (Grijalva, 2015).

A moderate level of narcissism is needed for effective leadership

The consideration here is at what point the level of narcissism has a negative impact on the behaviours of employees, thereby creating an employer brand that is out of alignment with the desired corporate brand. Emily Grijalva's study showed that although narcissists are more likely to emerge as group leaders, after a certain point, too much narcissism is likely to undermine a person's effectiveness as a leader.

The study's co-author Peter Harms, a professor of management in the College of Business Administration at the University of Nebraska, said those with moderate levels of narcissism have achieved 'a nice balance between having sufficient levels of self-confidence, but do not manifest the negative, antisocial aspects of narcissism that involve putting others down to feel good about themselves' (Reed, 2014).

Of course, some employees will relate to narcissistic leaders differently and more positively than others. However, the important point here is that those who emerge as leaders in an organization have a degree of narcissism – it is the management of this to appropriate levels that will ensure that it does not adversely affect relationships with employees and influence bad behaviours and employee brand.

Remember, self-confidence and optimism are healthy; arrogance and megalomania are not. Make sure you get the balance right.

Nothing is off the record

Much as when talking to a journalist nothing is ever off the record, the small actions and supposedly casual comments of the CEO or senior leaders aren't either. Eyes are always on you. When you're feeling under pressure or down because of some business adversity, you simply cannot show this. The ripple effect among your immediate leadership team, employees and even the media in the worst case, cannot be underestimated. So how do you balance this with remaining authentic? One answer is to be confident in yourself. Whatever happens is beyond your control but you can control how you deal with it and react to it. If you look back on your past, there are sure to be major challenges you have encountered. At the time these appeared to be massive challenges, but the chances are looking back they weren't so bad and you managed through them. This kind of mindset will help you to project an authentic confidence rather than a false one, keep your brand intact and avoid unnecessary turbulence in the company. How you person-ally manage through adversity is critical to keeping the company brand on track.

The power of line managers

Line managers can be your biggest area of concern (and opportunity) and create the most significant gap for leakage of brand messaging. This is often a middle management position that we regularly find does not receive the level of management training required in order to lead a team effectively. Quite often, line managers are promoted into their role organically without necessarily being totally ready for or qualified for the role. It is a role that is often filled by those who have been in the team the longest, understand the technical aspects, have been moved from another department, but have little or no training on how to authentically lead a team. I find from our work with organizations that often line managers do not reinforce the importance of adhering to a set of expected behaviours or 'live the brand' in a way that encourages and invites their team members to do the same. When delivering our programmes, we experience situations where we're told that an individual cannot attend a pre-organized coaching session or a training module due to being called out by their line manager. It even occasionally happens during coaching sessions – imagine the impact of this in terms of valuing and respecting the individual's personal development. Inexperienced line managers are more likely to migrate to and adopt a conscious or unconscious 'command and control' style of leadership rather than a coaching style of management that is more conducive to keeping the team on-board and feeling valued and respected. This can be due to lack of training and mentoring in how to lead effectively and is therefore a natural result of not having the basics of good leadership and influencing style in place. As we saw in Chapter 3, creating a strong team brand can help bridge this gap and provide your middle managers with the tools they need.

In Chapter 3 we looked at the Asda model for employee engagement. They recognize that challenges with employee engagement can be localized at line management level so they closely monitor and manage this with their employee engagement surveys.

Hayley Tatum, senior vice president of people and stores at Asda says that line managers are measured not just on their last three stock results (as is usually the case in retail), or in other words how controlled and accountable their retail routine is, but they are also measured on how engaging their leadership is. A leadership index is created for them so they can clearly see how they perform overall against the four pledges they have for employee engagement, against their peer group and the average for their grade. The line managers are keen to see these results from the surveys, and therefore they have a greater incentive to encourage their teams to complete the survey. They give them time in work hours to do this.

Hayley and her team can also clearly see from the surveys, although anonymous, if there is generally low performance in a particular area and can then work out which line manager needs to be focused on. Alternatively, of course, they can identify where celebration of achievement is deserved. It also enables her to focus their training and development efforts in the right areas and make investment where it is most needed, creating bespoke programmes, rather than making huge assumptions of what training is needed and in which areas.

Personal branding should start in the boardroom

The brand of your leadership team is now a significant element of your corporate brand messaging. Your employees look for a strong connection between your leadership brand and style, and the messaging of the company. Some 55 per cent of global executives who see their CEO as almost exclusively focused on the bottom line, see them also as having a weak reputation internally (Weber Shandwick, 2015). Employees need to see a strong personal brand from their leaders focusing on ethics, visibility and authenticity as well as profit margins.

With Generation Y and Generation Z coming into your organizations in force, you will find this will increasingly become the case as the next few years unfold. A common trait and perhaps expectation of Generation Y is to see people as equal. They dislike and won't work well under any indication of old-style command and control leadership styles. They will not automatically respect authority or leadership, just because of hierarchy, because they feel respect is personally earned. Senior leadership will therefore in their eyes not be exempt from the behaviours expected of the rest of the employee base. They come from a place of fairness and equality and if this is not demonstrated they will ultimately decide your company is not for them.

Leaders who make a personal connection with employees and show interest in their personal and career aspirations, inspire the highest levels of achievement among their teams. If people are valued, their productivity increases. If they are supported by a leader who they feel truly cares for them as an individual, then they have an ability to do more, achieve more and be more successful. These are all elements of your leadership brand that you need to take on-board to encourage a greater degree of employee engagement and ultimately influence a great employer brand and culture.

We need leaders with strong personal brands

We are starting to see a greater level of desire for recruiting leaders who have a strong personal brand already and who are known for their expertise in their specific field. Some forward-thinking companies now encourage their leaders to be more visible externally, including on social media, as they see it as a benefit to not just the leader themselves but the company also. I interviewed Andrew Grill, global managing partner at IBM Social Consulting, and he said his already strong personal brand in the marketplace in which he is known enabled him to put a price on what he was worth to IBM during the final interview stage. Andrew said that IBM sees a direct benefit to the business with him being 'out there and visible' and being considered a thought-leader in his own right. Andrew now recruits leaders into his team that have strong personal brands, as he's seen first-hand the benefits this brings to the business.

The benefits that can be expected from recruiting leaders with strong personal brands, and helping others to develop theirs are:

- more opportunities to get the corporate brand messaging out externally via a human interface;
- enhancement of employer brand and in particular in attracting Generation Y talent;
- increase in trust of the company (as the leader is willing to put himself on a stage and personally talk about the company and its value set);
- increase in authenticity and respect.

Here are some thoughts on how you might internally build your leadership brand and informally engage with your employees on a more personal level, along with the more formal elements of appraisals, performance reviews and rewards:

- modelling desired behaviours;
- meaningful connections and follow-through with actions and promises;
- adopting a coaching culture;

- creating forums and discussion groups for new ideas or to find solutions to challenges;
- gaining their input to the physical office environment;
- creating communities for topics and areas of interest, outside of the immediate scope of the business;
- relevant and meaningful team-building events that go beyond go-karting and paint-balling, and meet the needs of all team members, rather than alienating some of them;
- sharing your own stories of career development, adversity or challenge.

You can also ask yourself these questions to ascertain the effectiveness of your leadership brand. Wherever possible, you should also get feedback from others, as this may differ from your own perceptions and evaluations.

- Am I open and flexible to the different personalities and opinions of my team?
- Do I always provide honest, helpful and considered feedback to help develop my team members?
- Do I effectively give time to coach my team members to help their career development?
- When I look at myself in the mirror, do I feel a deep level of contentment with my leadership style and abilities?
- Have I given a high visibility project to a team member?
- Do I consistently recognize great performance?
- Do I fully understand the strengths and talents of all my team members and manage them accordingly?

A change in culture will take a great deal of time and effort to realize, of course. However, I hear a lot of talk about this in some of the companies I work with and those I'd like to, but in reality there are few companies and leadership teams that actually have the energy or capacity to make it happen. The CEO and executive team will often make the statement or create the strategy for the change required and believe the middle managers are behind them. The true picture is often that they are very far behind them and they do not have the buy-in they thought they had. An extremely visionary leadership is required in order to make big change and this is based on transparency and inclusion. Don't just assume that all your managers are in alignment with your thinking without putting in the effort to create this.

When I asked UK CEO of Handelsbanken, Anders Bouvin, what he believes his role is at Handelsbanken, he replied, 'My role is one of coach and supporter. I ensure that it is made as easy as possible within our branches for them to serve their customers in the way they believe is appropriate.' This demonstrates leadership at its best – create the values and the vision, ensure that local managers are clear on it via coaching and an open door, and then give them the power at the local level to run with it in their teams. Simple really, but the difficult part is putting in the energy to effect it.

Putting humour into the personality of the brand

We know that many of the most successful brands have humour or fun at their heart, for example Southwest Airlines and Virgin Atlantic. Herb Kelleher, co-founder and former CEO of Southwest Airlines said, 'What we are looking for, first and foremost, is a sense of humour. We hire attitudes.'

This is of course not a requirement to be successful, but it is certainly an asset for a brand to have a sense of humour associated with it. We can see that in recent years, fun and humour has become an integral part of TV advertising – Specsavers have made a whole brand out of their entertaining and funny advertisements. This has been achieved to such a level that the 'Should have gone to Specsavers' tagline has become a widely recognized punchline for everyday situations, certainly in the United Kingdom. Generation Y are known to be more attracted to brands that have humorous advertising so it's a sensible route to go down.

You may be thinking, 'That's fine for *those* companies, but that could never work here because our brand is very high class and we cater to a very professional and serious clientele.'

Fair enough, and we know the key to effective branding is to be congruent with the values you have created. But this doesn't mean there isn't room for any humour, especially since all we're really talking about is adding a human voice to your branding efforts and making a human connection with people. Mike Kerr, president of Humour at Work and author of *The Humour Advantage*, says 'No matter how serious your business or how serious you think your customers are, there's *always* a little room for some safe humour' (Kerr, 2015).

The use of humour can also help businesses brand themselves as attractive places to work and do business. Companies such as Zappos, the online shoes and clothing retailer, attract new employees in numbers far exceeding their competitors because they've branded themselves as a fun and positive place to work. On listening to Jenn Lim, CEO and chief happiness officer at Delivering Happiness and a Zappos consultant, speak at a conference recently I heard how they have created a 'Happiness Framework' that serves to create a culture that all employees at Zappos clearly understand and follow. In fact, it is grounds for firing if employees are not contributing to the culture. The Happiness Framework consists of:

- perceived control;
- perceived progress;
- connectedness;
- vision/meaning (being part of something bigger than yourself).

Other companies use humour to attract customers and turn those customers into raving, passionate fans for their business. Humour works so effectively as a branding tool because it helps make any business more likeable; it humanizes even large, conservative companies. Humour also builds good-will capital that companies can draw upon when things go off the rails.

Paul E ter Wal, engagement and accountability expert from the Netherlands says, 'Happiness has a direct relationship with work engagement. Happy people have more personal energy and when they also work in a stimulating environment with more responsibility, more resources, feedback etc, they will get more energy from their work as well. So, there will be an increased employee engagement. Higher work engagement will have a significant impact on productivity and profitability of an organization.'

Phil Jones, managing director of Brother UK uses 'Alacrity – a happy state of readiness', to describe the business culture he tries to create at Brother UK. He says, 'It's what a modern workplace needs to be. Alacrity addresses the human conditions and resiliency needed to be responsive in a disruptive world, which ultimately then leads to business agility.'

Humour or fun is increasingly being recognized as a core business value that both drives success and reflects success. Beyond the obvious benefits of humour in the workplace as a tool for boosting morale, strengthening relationships and managing stress, we know from numerous studies that humour also improves trust in the workplace, facilitates better communication, increases productivity, lowers employee absenteeism, and it's a huge catalyst for creativity and innovation.

Of course, the humour you use as a company needs to be congruent with your brand. If you have a classy brand, then your humour, for the most part, should be classy. If you want to be known as an edgy company, then use edgy humour. Make sure the fun aspects contribute to and reflect the brand image you want to project, both personally and as a company.

Top leaders, starting at the CEO level, set the tone for any organization and if humour or fun is a core value for you, then it's imperative that senior leaders lead by example and demonstrate a willingness to laugh at themselves. Embracing a sense of humour is one of the most effective ways to make a leader more genuine and more human, and it's a key way to build trust. Because humour helps leaders become more likeable and therefore more approachable, it's also a principal way to build a culture of open and honest communication.

> Appropriate humour is a great way to build trust

This doesn't mean the CEO has to adopt a habit of wearing Mickey Mouse socks or morph into Jerry Seinfeld or Joan Rivers during their next business presentation. Nor does it mean they have to be an extrovert or exude fake enthusiasm. Many CEOs in organizations that embrace a sense of fun and humour are in fact introverts. Embracing a sense of humour is rarely about being funny – it's about demonstrating that you are human and able to laugh at your own mishaps.

Mike Kerr provides these simple top tips for senior leaders to use to demonstrate a healthy sense of humour:

- First and foremost, don't squash the natural humour and fun that happens organically in most organizations.

- Admit when you mess up and show that you're willing to laugh at yourself. Share personal anecdotes that will help employees see the person behind the job title.

- Participate in team-building events, wacky theme days, employee skit nights, or funny video montages to demonstrate your willingness to 'go along' and poke a bit of fun at your own expense.

- Have an employee, or if you're really game, a child, interview you on video in a relaxed context that allows you to share some personal, fun insights about yourself.

- Whenever you address the troops don't try too hard to be funny (it can backfire painfully if this isn't natural for you), but do bring your openness and personality along for the ride.

- Share your early bloopers and blunders. Bloopers and even embarrassing stories are natural conduits for humour and sharing these kinds of stories will go a long way towards helping you build trust and come across as more genuine and human.

When it comes to humour, it's all about authenticity. The brands that make humour work are authentic; they know their persona and they run with it. Some companies sell mundane products, but using humour in their marketing has transformed the way consumers perceive them. For you as CEO or a senior leader in your company, you need to work on ways to add humour and fun in an appropriate way into your daily lives, team meetings, presentations, interviews and external events.

Here are just three ideas that provide a basis for some creative thought around introducing more fun into your environment:

- Start a team humour file or book where you collect funny customer questions and humorous, work-related material. A humour file reminds everyone to sharpen their humour saw and it serves as a repository for material that you can share during meetings, on your intranet site, or on a humour bulletin board.

- Encourage managers to create alternative job titles for their team that celebrate the true nature of their work. For example, 'Queen of fun and laughter' or 'Director of first impressions'. Even consider having these printed on the back of business cards. It's a fun talking point.

- Humour drives creativity, so make sure your meetings are fun. Add a humour break to the middle of a long meeting or kick off your meetings with a fun tradition.

Whatever methods you use to bring more fun and humour into your workplace, they need to be congruent with your personal brand as a senior leader. Remember you set the scene or level for others. If you're unsure how to approach this, select a group of people to discuss some ideas, or bring in a humorist like Mike Kerr to assist. It's such an important element of getting personality into your brand today, that you really don't want to overlook it.

Executive presence

This is often a term bandied about in business and a 'state' coveted by learning and development managers from their leaders. But what does it actually mean and why is it important? In my view it's about how people feel about you as soon as you enter a room or start a meeting or presentation and the confidence they have in you, the credibility you exude from your non-verbal communication and then your content and delivery. It's about your ability to inspire others to contribute to their fullest potential, and to be valued in what they bring to the table. Leaders with great executive presence have the ability to access their intuition and trust it, be agile and remain open to others' views and ideas, and to learning.

You can improve your executive presence by:

- using your senses more and assessing how others are feeling or where they stand before you respond;
- being authentic and true to your values;
- being as self-aware as possible and actively seeking ways to do this;
- communicating clearly.

When we look at building your personal brand in Chapter 5, you will see other ways of improving your executive presence while remaining true to yourself.

Assess your leadership brand

There are many ways in which to influence a culture shift and we know it can take a while. However, your brand and behaviours at leadership level are crucial for providing guidance and the inspiration to the entire employee base for them to emulate in their own individual way. Be careful about aligning your own behaviours closely with what you are trying to achieve at corporate brand level and encourage a strong feedback culture to ensure you are keeping on-message and not deviating without realizing it. This is the only way you can effectively manage your brand as a leader.

As an action point, ask a selected cross-section of your managers and employees the following questions of your leadership brand:

- What is most inspirational about our leadership here?
- What are the three things that need to change in order for us to fully represent and reinforce the corporate brand at leadership level?

In summary, be under no illusion that your personal brand as a leader is not pivotal to the brand of your company. Treat it with the enthusiastic focus and importance you and your company deserve.

It is important to act on the feedback you gather above, and we'll be covering more on how to map this and other feedback over your authentic personal brand in Chapter 5, Getting back on-message.

References

George, B (2004) *Authentic Leadership Rediscovering the Secrets to Creating Lasting Value*, John Wiley & Sons, San Francisco

George, B *et al* (2007) Discovering your authentic leadership, *Harvard Business Review*, February. Available from: https://hbr.org/2007/02/discovering-your-authentic-leadership [2015]

Grijalva, E *et al* (2015) Narcissism and leadership: a meta-analytic review of linear and nonlinear relationships, *Personnel Psychology*, **68**, 1–47

Jensen, A (2014) [accessed 10 October 2015] CEO pay and reputation, Burson-Marsteller Blog 4 December. Available from: http://burson-marsteller.ch/en/2014/12/ceo-pay-and-reputation/

Kerr, M (2015) *The Humor Advantage: Why some businesses are laughing all the way to the bank*, Humor at Work

Reed, L (2014) [accessed 10 October 2015] Study examines link between narcissism, leadership quality, UNL Today, 16 January. Available from: http://news.unl.edu/newsrooms/unltoday/article/study-examines-link-between-narcissism-leadership-quality/

Weber Shandwick (2015) [accessed 10 October 2015] 'The CEO reputation premium: gaining advantage in the engagement era', Weber Shandwick. Available from: http://webcache.googleusercontent.com/search?q=cache:u49l-e75VPcJ:www.webershandwick.com/uploads/news/files/ceo-reputation-premium-executive-summary.pdf+&cd=1&hl=en&ct=clnk&gl=uk

Getting back on-message

05

Now the real work begins. By this point, you will quite likely have taken mental stock at least of where your company is on the scale of balance of corporate brand and how your people reflect that brand from an employer and employee brand perspective. You will be able to see more clearly where the danger areas are and what needs to be measured and addressed. You will also have a more conscious appreciation of the impact that people behaviour and leadership style have on your customer and stakeholder experience. The level to which these behaviours directly impact how your brand is talked about internally and externally, and globally via social media in particular, will have become more apparent.

Now's the time to look at how to approach the people brand challenge. Here we look at:

- what corporate culture really is;
- the real corporate branding process;
- achieving changes in behaviours by looking at the personal brand of people;
- the Walking TALL principles;
- the espresso effect;
- celebrity brand me;
- building rapport with other personality types;
- roll-out of a brand training experience;
- keeping momentum;
- introducing your brand me map.

Let's see how you can address these areas and bring about a greater degree of balance between what you are advertising and promising that you stand for and what your leadership team and your people actually represent on a daily basis. This is the only way to consistently create more trust, respect and authenticity in your organization.

Consistency is not optional

I mentioned in Chapter 2 my interview with Richard Branson. One area I was interested in was how he viewed personal image. Over the years people had said to me, well look at Branson – he doesn't dress well and he often looks a little shabby, even for formal presentations; he doesn't present very well, and his eye contact when he's interviewed is terrible. But he's been very successful – what do you have to say about that? Therefore, one of the questions I asked Branson was: 'For a person who I know is very particular about image within your Virgin Group of companies, you seem to break a lot of the image rules yourself – what do you put your success down to?' His reply was this: 'When I started out in business in the City of London 30 or so years ago, everybody was in their pinstripe suits, their bowler hats and had long lunches in private clubs. I broke conformity. And when you break conformity to that degree, how can you fail to succeed?'

Powerful answer isn't it? However, I believe his success goes deeper – it is the *consistency* with which he breaks conformity that is a key to his success. He can only be consistent because he is being truly authentic in everything he does. It is what he knows and does best because it comes naturally to him, therefore he can continually behave in this way. It is when we get to this level of clarity of our authentic brand that we can become highly consistent with how we project ourselves, and therefore take others with us much more effectively. This is a necessary discipline in leadership today.

A change in behaviour is required

Before we can attempt to change behaviours, there needs to be a thorough understanding of the existing behaviours and culture at every level. Then a re-defining of corporate values must take place to a level of clarity that can be understood and clearly deployed throughout the organization. This is where many companies fail to achieve the desired outcomes – lack of clarity at senior level leads to confusion and reduced levels of engagement by the whole company, with the ultimate dilution of corporate brand investment. Brand agencies are often employed to assist with and/or create a new brand, a new feel to the organization or a heightened customer experience. As wonderful as they are in achieving this at top level, most companies then fall short at communicating this in straightforward language and with techniques that their entire employee base can understand and implement. In addition, the people most often at the cutting edge of the customer experience are those at the lower end of the management scale and who traditionally receive less behavioural training than others. Yet they are in direct contact with clients and customers every single day, creating a customer experience, positive or negative, many times over. The most powerful customer touch-points are in the hands of people you spend the least amount of training budget on per capita and I would suggest perhaps neglect in terms of value and respect.

So what is corporate culture?

We need to know what is meant by 'corporate culture' before we can address it. It can mean a number of things; however, I believe most importantly it includes a clear vision and value set, clarity of expectations around that vision and value set, and people and a set of attitudes, behaviours and practices that reinforce the same. A culture is portrayed across a number of communication mediums – verbal and non-verbal – and we could say that it is 'the way things are done around here'.

Written codes may be written for some of these areas too, for example behaviour guidelines and dress codes. Many times I have witnessed a written dress code that leaves it open to many different interpretations. Yet a company will consider that because it has a dress code everybody will follow it and interpret it in the way the person writing it has intended. In my experience, this is not so. There will instead be a 'trend' of dress that will become reflected eventually by all. If a standard is set by line managers and senior leadership for the dress code to be casual, then that dress style will tend to be adopted by the rest of the organization, perhaps to a more extreme degree. If the CEO is well dressed, sharp and well coordinated, then this standard is likely to be reflected by his executive team and senior leaders, resulting in filtering down to others in various teams. On the other hand, if the CEO or any of the executive team are sloppy in their dress style, this will not only get talked about widely, but will tend to spark a subconscious thought process of 'I don't need to worry about my shirt not fitting well, or my shoes not being clean, the CEO won't even notice'. Thereafter an element of culture is created.

Likewise, I notice in dealing with organizations that if I experience a lack of communication or responses to e-mails with one person, it is likely to be similar with others. Or perhaps a tendency not to turn up for phone meetings that have been arranged will often be repeated by others. Subconsciously this behaviour has spread internally, and a culture has been created. Ultimately, a culture is created by the consistent behaviours of people. So in order to create the desired culture you need a plan to effect behavioural change that really works.

Putting the plan into practice

Of course having a clear brand strategy is vital; however, that is not what this book is about. I'm assuming you have the strategy already. What we will deal with is creating the right culture to allow this strategy to be rolled out effectively, take your internal brand engagement to another level and ultimately ensure you achieve what you need to with your brand messaging, both internally and externally.

We've established in Chapter 4, that any change needs to be supported and reflected by the leaders, and encouraged to develop by line managers and their teams. Let's now look at how to implement a programme that will truly effect change in behaviours and create a greater level of engagement with the corporate brand, with the ultimate result of high levels of positive customer experience and consistency.

The only real way to effect change is to get to the heart and mindset of the individual. If we can provide a framework and methodology for *all* individuals to follow that encourages authenticity, self-awareness of strengths and brand, and an environment that positively promotes and supports individual reinforcement of the corporate brand values, then we get results. I cannot stress enough, if you are to get the much-needed results you need to engage the entire employee base with these principles.

Too often, minimal training is given in the actual *how to* of projecting and reinforcing the values, and not only externally to customers and clients, but also behaviours internally among employees at all levels. This is because values have to be about the individual, not the company, in order for an individual to internalize them and 'live' them.

Even though we find that most of our clients are now moving back towards training programmes with an element of intimate and face-to-face medium for training, you may not have the luxury of putting every single employee through a training programme such as this. If you can, then you will have a much greater chance of full engagement and success. By face to face I don't just mean a company-wide conference, with a big stage, lights and huge hype. Gone are the days when events like this alone would truly engage employees to the level needed to effect change. I'm not disregarding company-wide conferences; indeed I present the Walking TALL message at many – however, we need to follow through with a greater degree of engagement and momentum than conferences alone can achieve. This is why I developed the Walking TALL methodology that will enable you to achieve a level of engagement with corporate values among your people that you've not reached before.

So let's now look at the suggested steps required in order to start really addressing the people projection of the corporate brand for your organization.

The real corporate branding process

First, you need to ascertain where you're at now and where the gaps are between your desired corporate brand messaging and the reality of the customer experience. What needs to be fixed in order for the brand investment to be maximized and the dilution to be limited? While this book is focused on the people behaviours and personal branding elements, I have mentioned below in overview, other elements that need to be extracted and highlighted from the complete brand process to achieve the ultimate results.

Stage 1 – Get total clarity on your brand values

I'm assuming here that you have carried out a level of work on establishing your corporate brand values, either by working with an agency, or internally with your marketing and executive teams, and now want to roll out the

FIGURE 5.1 The real corporate branding process

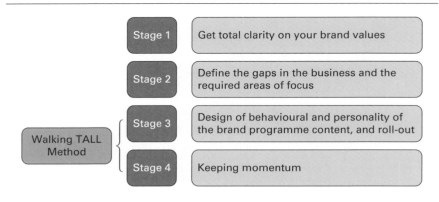

brand messaging, or reinforce it as effectively as possible throughout your employee base. Many of our clients work with us after a re-brand or a re-focus on the existing brand to take company-wide engagement as deep as possible, but first you need to have some clarity on your vision and values and how you want your customers and stakeholders to feel when they experience your brand.

Ask yourself, are the values really meaningful, achievable and able to be easily understood by all levels of staff? Are they really embedded in your vision or are they just words? Can you truly achieve what you promise? The demise of Enron in 2001 was down to uncovering unethical practices and bad financial reporting. However, it's interesting to note that their values as stated on their website at the time were:

Respect: We treat others as we would like to be treated ourselves. We do not tolerate abusive or disrespectful treatment. Ruthlessness, callousness and arrogance don't belong here.

Integrity: We work with customers and prospects openly, honestly and sincerely. When we say we will do something, we will do it; when we say we cannot or will not do something, we won't do it.

Communication: We have an obligation to communicate. Here, we take the time to talk with one another... and to listen. We believe that information is meant to move and that information moves people.

Excellence: We are satisfied with nothing less than the very best in everything we do. We will continue to raise the bar for everyone. The great fun here will be for all of us to discover just how good we can really be.

We can clearly see that not all company values are truly believed in and reinforced with passion and authenticity by the leadership team.

As a leadership team, you need to spend some time gathering input from a cross-section of staff (levels, age, customer-facing, back office), on how they perceive the brand and what it might mean to them in terms of their behaviours. This will help you to gain an appreciation for the level of understanding you have in the company, the consistency and where the focus needs to be.

Great questions to ask your teams to aid this might be:

● In your view, what would you say the company brand attempts to project to our customers?

● How do you interpret this in terms of your everyday role and how you need to behave?

Create and encourage discussion forums to discuss these areas.

Then establish in clear language, how you want to be perceived, in a manner that can easily be understood by all employees. However, don't think it ends there. This is the mistake a lot of companies make – 'We have the clarity of the brand values and now all we need to do is communicate them out with widgets, posters and sheep-dip type training courses on values.' This is the danger area – stopping here will not achieve what you need to achieve with getting into the mindsets of all employees, truly engaging them and changing their everyday behaviours and interactions with others.

I would strongly suggest that during your brand strategy planning phase, you include plans for a focused programme and budget for how you are going to bring your entire employee base on-board with consistent messages, total understanding of what the objectives are and most importantly provide them with the tools to internalize the values and make the changes.

Stage 2 – Define the gaps in the business and the required areas of focus

Having gained clarification on the brand messaging and the level and depth of engagement needed by your leaders, managers and whole employee base to achieve the goals, we now need to look at what specific personal branding traits, behaviours and attitudes need to be addressed. This can be gained from your line managers and clients alike. Analyse from your customer surveys what is missing most from the experience they receive that can be addressed with changes in behaviours.

Some of the typical areas of focus that you may be seeing as needed might include:

- personal ownership of what the brand means to me;
- self-confidence in all interactions;
- understanding of what a customer needs from their experience with our company;
- self-awareness and perceptions that others have of me;
- appreciation that people buy people and that I make the difference;
- visibility internally and externally;
- profile building;
- building rapport with all personality types;
- professional presence;
- personal impact and executive polish.

The above are the typical areas of focus that our clients come to us with when looking specifically at how they can create a powerful reinforcement and projection of the brand via their people. A suitable tailored programme can then be developed to address these areas.

Stage 3 – Design of behavioural and personality of the brand programme content, and roll-out

For each community within your business, you will need to ascertain the approach to take, the content and the delivery mechanisms to make the greatest amount of impact. As mentioned earlier, while big company-wide conferences can achieve a level of awareness, they are rarely enough to embed the personal brand principles needed to motivate and effect change in individuals. A blended approach may be needed, and in my experience is most effective for achieving the desired results.

Stage 4 – Keeping momentum

Having delivered effective programmes that provide the right tools and motivation to individuals to create a change in behaviours, you now need to keep this mindset alive. It can so easily slip back into the category of 'old habits die hard'. This needs the buy-in from line managers in particular, as they represent the closest influence on the majority of the workforce.

The Walking TALL principles

I have created a journey for personal branding that helps individuals create a brand that is in alignment with and reflects your corporate branding. It provides a golden thread that keeps them on track, with specific outputs along the way.

The Walking TALL principles address Stages 3 and 4 in particular, so we're going to explore those in more detail now. My aim here is to take you through the methodology in detail so you can apply the thinking and tools to yourself initially, with a view to rolling this out company-wide. We have seven key areas of focus, or principles for defining and building a personal brand that we call 'seven big strides to personal branding'. Here they are in overview and the content of each will be covered in this chapter, and also in Chapters 6 and 7.

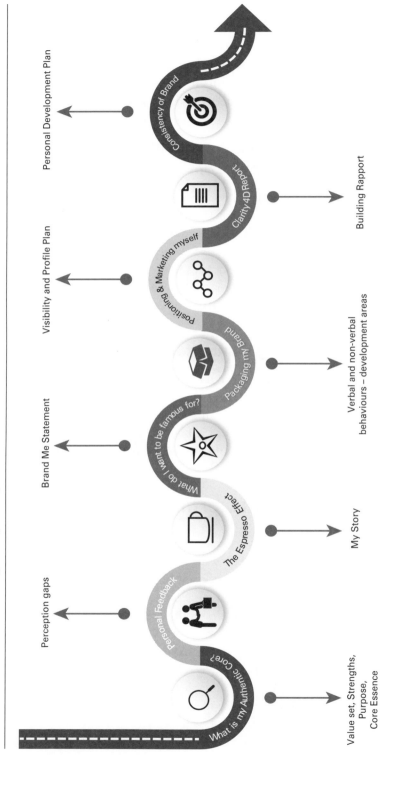

FIGURE 5.2 The Walking TALL journey

Personal Development Plan

Visibility and Profile Plan

Brand Me Statement

Perception gaps

Consistency of Brand

Clarity4D Report

Positioning & Marketing myself

Packaging my Brand

What do I want to be famous for?

The Espresso Effect

Personal Feedback

What is my Authentic Core?

Building Rapport

Verbal and non-verbal behaviours – development areas

My Story

Value set, Strengths, Purpose, Core Essence

1 Who you really are
This is the starting point. A strong personal brand has to be authentic so that it can be more easily maintained and sustained.

2 Right from the outset
It only takes a few seconds to make a first impression and many interactions for it to be changed.

3 Visual brand counts
Whether we like it or not, our non-verbal communication (dress and body language) give clues away as to our personality in the eyes of the beholder.

4 Be memorable and visible
We need to create a profile and visibility plan to consciously manage our exposure within our target market.

5 Presentational brand matters
Becoming great at presenting an authentic message is a crucial element of our brand.

6 Statement 'brand me'
We need to be able to define our personal brand in a few powerful sentences that become our brand statement.

7 Each time, all the time
Consistency is the key to success with any brand, particularly a personal brand. Without this we only create confusing messages.

The complete personal brand

A personal brand consists of layers, but for it to be truly unique and sustainable it needs to start with the authentic core and then be built from the inside out. The authentic core is supported and represented by your values, strengths and purpose in life. You then need to package your brand to project this core authenticity consistently with every interaction. The outer ring then serves to keep your brand visible and prominent and is an ongoing process. Often when coaching individuals at senior level, I find that the outer ring is incongruent with the inner core. People become 'moulded' over time by the outside world, and subconsciously behave in a way that they think is expected of them to a level that moves them away from who they really are. Now is the time to stop and re-align your brand. Strip the layers away back to the core, and build them up again more strategically and purposefully, in alignment with who you really are.

FIGURE 5.3   The complete personal brand

Think like an entrepreneur

Your personal brand is what people say about you behind your back

We have a personal brand already, whether we've consciously developed it or not. Your brand is quite simply what others say about you behind your back and the collection of powerful and clear ideas they have about you when they think of you or recommend you to others. You cannot afford to leave this perception to chance anymore – you need to take conscious control of your brand and manage your own personal PR and marketing more like an entrepreneur than ever before. Even after you've defined your personal brand, it takes evaluating on a continuous basis in order to sustain it. People will create their own brand for you in their minds and if you create confusing messages you're not making it easy for them to talk about you in the way you need them to because it's authentic. In *The Picture of Dorian Gray*, Oscar Wilde said, 'There's only one thing in the world worse than being talked about, and that's not being talked about.' Today, we need to be talked about, but we need to take control over what those messages might be. In fact if people don't talk about us we are pretty invisible and will lose out on opportunities for recognition, exposure and promotion. In his book *The Purple Cow* (2005), Seth Godin talks about being 'remarkable' – our brand needs to create a memorable impact on others, in a positive sense of course, in order for us to remain relevant and visible. We'll talk more about visibility in Chapter 6, Raising your visibility factor.

Whether your aim is to build name or expert recognition in your field, build more visibility with your target market and/or influence others as a high-profile leader, then you need to understand the key principles involved and take control of the perceptions others have of you.

The single most important part of personal branding to realize is, that in order for it to be authentic and sustainable, it needs to be created from the inside out. Your brand is not something you invent; it needs to be defined from your very core. You need to 'put on the brakes', take time to consider, reflect and assess your brand, and then build the layers that will package and project that brand every day with every interaction. This way, you create a consistent message for yourself that others can easily remember, talk about and recommend. Did you ever meet somebody who seemed to have a natural ability to attract, listened to you easily, was engaged in your conversation and you felt was comfortable in their own shoes? Then this was probably a person who not only has a strong personal brand but also understands clearly what their brand is. Being authentic in who you are acts as a powerful magnet. It's the consistency that builds the trust.

A few years ago, a good friend of mine recommended a designer for a piece of artwork I needed creating. His words to me were: 'Bill is great, but he won't return your e-mails or phone calls, is totally disorganized, looks a mess but is superb at his job.' Because one of my strong values is responsiveness, this was a complete no-no for me, but I did think what an interesting set of words he used to 'sell and market' Bill to me. It's imperative today to know what people are saying about you behind your back.

The pearl effect

Imagine a pearl in an oyster – it grows organically over a period of time as layers get added to it. This is similar to your corporate brand and your personal brand as an individual. Every customer touch-point or personal interaction you have, verbal and non-verbal, creates a layer that over time defines your brand and reputation in the eyes of others. Every e-mail you send, every text, presentation, meeting or chat at lunch, adds a layer to your brand and it gradually evolves.

It is quite common for us to be unclear about whether the layers added are reinforcing our brand positively and consistently, or whether they are weakening and diluting the brand. This is due to two things – the lack of clarity about what the brand actually is whether corporate or personal, and because we don't think about it or measure it consistently. The pearl analogy can help us to keep on track and create a conscious focus in our minds as to the messages we want others to know about us and think about us as our brand. Without this line of thinking, it is difficult to remain conscious of our brand and keep adding the layers in a strategic or perhaps deliberate way.

The brand tree

There are many analogies we can use for personal branding; however, the tree and its hidden roots explain it well. Often hidden beneath the surface are our true values, our character traits, our strengths, drivers, beliefs and purpose. Others don't see them clearly because they are hidden or obscured, yet they represent the DNA of our brand or our authentic core. Others don't see them clearly because you don't project them consistently and I would suggest you are not entirely clear about them yourself either. We don't tend to spend time on defining our values or what our brand stands for; therefore it is very often left to chance.

The branches and the leaves of the tree represent the visible elements of our brand – people see these every day and judge us on them. Elements such as our appearance, body language, voice, interaction with others, attitude, written communication, social skills and presentational skills are seen, experienced, talked about and in turn create perceptions about us every day. These perceptions can be slightly or significantly 'off-message' with our actual authentic brand.

So in order to create an authentic brand image, we need to discover our brand elements at our core, our true DNA, and assemble all the pieces to

FIGURE 5.4   The brand tree

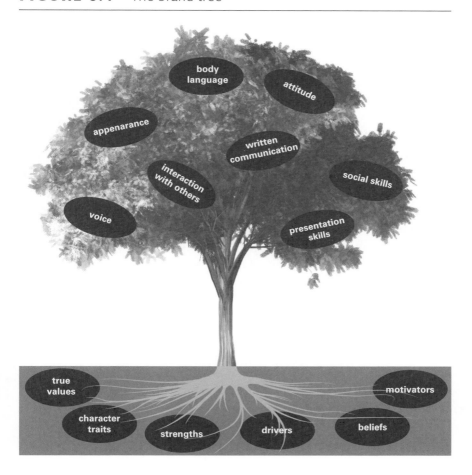

create the full picture. We'll work through the process to achieve this later in this chapter.

Coming from a place of authenticity

'Be clear and transparent with your values'

Nobody can operate from their authentic core if their values are regularly compromised. In order to really appreciate if these values are being compromised of course, we need to clarify what our values really are. If I ask you now to write down your top five personal values, would you be able to without thinking for too long? Chances are you probably can't do this, because you don't spend time on defining what is really important to you. If you're not personally clear about what your values are, others around you won't be either. In order to take others with you and to lead effectively, you need to be transparent with your values and consistent in the projection of them. Ask yourself if there is a potential gap here.

In terms of your corporate brand values, in order for you and your people to reflect these you need to know how they translate to you personally and how you can reinforce them authentically in your everyday interactions and behaviours. Take a corporate brand value that is often cited – integrity. This means something different to different people. Write down three words that for you describe the word integrity. Ask the rest of your leadership team what it means for them. You'll very likely find that you all have different definitions of the same word. Do this exercise with each of your corporate brand values and see what you get. You're likely to find that there is a completely diverse set of words as individuals interpret the values in their own way. This is exactly what is needed – for people to really 'live the brand' they need to understand what it means to them. However, what must happen next is that individuals need to be given the tools to be able to analyse how they can use their personal brand in their everyday work to reinforce the corporate values in a meaningful way for them. If you can achieve this, your level of engagement with the values is enhanced significantly across the company.

Defining your personal brand basics

So now's the time to take time out to think about your personal brand and what you want to be known for or 'famous' for. Remember, others create a brand for you in their minds which may be totally incongruent with your authentic core, how you see yourself and how you want to be perceived. Your brand will evolve over a period of time but now we're going to put the foundations in place for you to build on, reinforce and project with every interaction you have.

Imagine for a few minutes, looking at yourself in a hypothetical full-length mirror. When you look at the 'brand' you see, what words would you use to describe your 'brand me'? Use the chart in Figure 5.5 to plot the key words that you feel describe your authentic brand. Don't use any feedback you've been given by others at this stage – it is important for you to focus on your brand as you see it. One important point here – keep it positive!

FIGURE 5.5   Personal brand profile

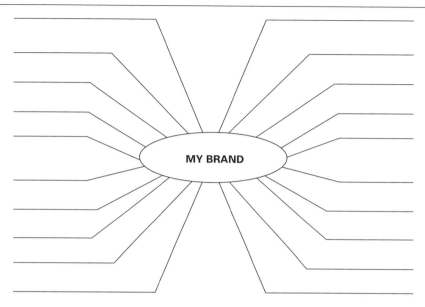

While I'm not suggesting that you ignore negative traits, at this point we're going to focus on how you want to project yourself. Let me give you some thoughts around how to extract the pertinent words for your brand.

Consider these particular areas:

- your personality;
- talents and strengths;
- natural style.

Don't try to put words into the specific categories – this is just an open 'brain dump' onto the sheet. Talents and strengths are tough to define – what you're good at is invisible to you, therefore you don't value it. Others can see what you're good at often more clearly than you. Think about what you do every day that you just get on and do, but may actually reflect a talent.

What you're good at is invisible to you, therefore you don't value it

Once, when coaching a senior lawyer, we were talking about what she does as part of her role in order to establish visibility and profile. She mentioned that she often gets asked to write an article for the firm's magazine, which indicated to me of course that she has a talent for writing. When I mentioned this her reaction was, 'I'm not good at writing, everybody's good at writing; I just do it because I enjoy doing it'! She did not recognize that she had a specific talent. These are the kinds of things I mean here – what do you just get on with not realizing it's a talent?

Determining values

Another element of your brand and arguably the most important are your values or principles. Values are often tough to define too; however, it is essential that you are clear about your value set in order to live in line with your authentic brand. These are your guiding principles in life.

Decisions in life and business become easier if you are clear about your values and what's important to you. If you make decisions in line with your values they will always be easier to make and most often be the right ones to make. If you look back in life and consider all the good and bad decisions you've ever made, you can pretty much be sure that the bad ones are out of alignment with your value set, and your good ones are aligned. Your values are unique to you – nobody else will have the same set as you – a bit like a values fingerprint. Here are some questions you can ask yourself to determine what your values are:

- How do you most like to spend your time and why?
- What do you get most of your energy from doing?
- What inspires you most?
- What do you set goals on most?
- What do you dream about most?
- What do you enjoy doing most, at work and at home?

In addition, you can ask yourself:

- What drives you mad about other people – what they do or don't do or say?

Often when you examine the things that affect you negatively or make you feel uncomfortable, you can ascertain what is important to you or what you believe in by turning it around. Take, for example, somebody who is always late for meetings; this drives you mad. I bet you always arrive early or on time for meetings but your personal value may be about respect for others' time, not punctuality per se. Or how about people who always seem to exaggerate to get noticed or make an impact – perhaps this one is about honesty or authenticity.

CASE STUDY

I recently worked with the CEO of a large public sector organization, who as part of the coaching programme was able to ascertain what drove her to where she is now, and this happened several years ago. At the age of 18, she was not the outgoing, outspoken and confident professional she is now. In fact she was very shy and quiet, and the thought of speaking in public was one of her biggest fears. When she was at high school, it was the time of year again when the applications for the next head girl were invited. It was never going to enter her head to apply, as it was a foregone conclusion who was going to get it – the attractive, blonde, bubbly girl who everybody loved. This didn't appear fair to my client, as she felt there were others who should be given the chance and could fulfil the role equally well or better. She had no idea what drove her to apply, but she did and she was elected into the position. From this point on she had to present to large school audiences regularly and found that she actually loved it and developed a skill for it. When we analysed what drove her to apply during the work we were doing on her values, it became clear that her highest value was fairness. That day she had totally acted in alignment with her strongest value without consciously recognizing it, and it was this decision that was instrumental to her success in business today.

Behave in alignment with your values

It may be a challenge for you to come up with your values. Here is a list of some to get you started. Feel free of course to add and change where necessary. Ideally, you need to end up with between 5 and 10.

- honesty;
- love;
- family;
- peace;
- fun;
- freedom;
- energy;
- learning;
- accomplishment;
- connection;
- integrity;
- pride;
- control;
- recognition;
- innovation;
- wealth;
- spirituality;
- community;
- order;
- creativity;
- being organized;
- security;
- practical;
- progress;
- experience;
- adventure.

When you've got your values clarified, you need to prioritize them. This can be difficult to do, so create scenarios in your mind to help. For example, if you're not sure what's more important between fun and peace – think about being faced with the option of a kayaking trip with friends or sitting in the quiet reading a book. What would you be more likely to opt for? This is obviously a choice in its simplest sense; however, bigger life choices can be made easier if you are clear about your values and their priorities.

You can now think about your day and much of it is aligned to your values. Do the same with your job and your life in general. If the things you find yourself doing most are not aligned to your top values then something probably feels unbalanced in your life. You need to get back on track. By writing these values down you will have made a good start on this process.

CASE STUDY

I recently worked with a female executive team member of a FTSE 250 company. She was well respected within the senior leadership team and the company as a whole. However, her confidence was being severely affected by consistent disregard for her career and emotional needs due to the CEO's constant lack of direction and changes regarding reporting structures and responsibilities on the board. It was a clear case of the CEO going down a constantly changing route without consultation and buy-in from the rest of the board. The negative impact of this on individuals is obvious. More and more changes in responsibility were being imposed on my client that directly attacked her personal values of collaboration, loyalty and fairness and this is where the problems started. Of course there is no going backwards when your values are compromised consistently, even though she may not have admitted or even realized this at the time. It is only through a gradual process that this becomes obvious, and then it is too late. It was this misalignment in the end that led her to resign and the company lost a hugely valuable senior executive in the process. This could so easily have been prevented had a level of respect for the individual been forthcoming. How often could this be happening in your organization and how much is it costing the bottom line?

Leadership values

Now look at all the words you've written down. If you were to create an authentic leadership brand for yourself, which words would be the most important to you? Which three to six words would you most like people to use about you behind your back as a leader? Put a circle around these now. How effectively would others say you are projecting these traits and values right now? Test this out with your direct reports – ask questions like:

- What should I do more of or less of to enable you to do your job as effectively as possible?
- How consistent is my leadership style?
- What motivates/demotivates you with my leadership style?

From the responses, you will be able to determine which elements of your desired leadership brand are lacking and which to capitalize on most.

Brand picture

You are starting to see that your brand is made up of many pieces that fit together, a bit like a jigsaw puzzle. However, this puzzle is unique – there is no other quite like it. The final view of the puzzle is the picture on the lid of the box or a visual of the brand you want to project. It is important for you to be clear about what that picture is so that you can bring all the pieces together to reflect that brand image.

Try also considering your brand as a bottle of wine – what would your label look like; what would it say; how would you stand out from all the others on the liquor store shelf? How would the back label read to describe you in a few sentences? It's a fun exercise to design your own label and what your brand may look like.

FIGURE 5.6   The brand me jigsaw

We can take this analogy further – what the French call the 'terroir', the sense of place, or the foundation of the wine, can be equated to your DNA, where you come from, your roots. The grapes give the wine its individual personality and flavour or characteristics – your values, your drivers and motivators, behaviours and talents. The final piece is the climate that nurtures the wine – the network you build, the skills you learn, your personal development. These elements become your real differentiators. All three elements are needed to create an authentic brand or a sustainable and robust bottle of wine!

Managing the perception gaps

So now you've got as much down as you can at this stage onto your chart, you need to start gauging where the gaps are between how you see yourself and how others perceive you. The best way to do this is by getting specific feedback from current and former colleagues, direct reports, your line managers and friends.

Ask questions like these:

- What three words would you use to describe me?
- What would you say my top values are?
- How do I come across to others?
- How do I come across on first impressions?
- What one behavioural trait would you change about me to improve the impact I make?

When you get the feedback, map it over the personal brand chart you have completed for yourself. You can use a highlighter pen to mark all those words that you have written down that are also coming through from others. These are the characteristics or brand values that you are most effectively projecting. Use another colour to mark all those words that nobody 'gets' about you. These are the areas that need the most attention – they are important to you and your authentic brand but nobody is seeing them strongly enough.

Keep a separate list of those words that people use to describe you that you don't see in yourself – your blind spots, both negative and positive. Consider if these are part of your authentic brand and should be added to your chart, or if they are perhaps false perceptions that need attention.

You will start to see where the common gaps are, ie the elements you see in yourself, your leadership values, the most important words to you, yet they are not coming through strongly enough from others. Create an action plan now for working on these specifics. As an example, if you see yourself as creative and this is important to you but doesn't come through clearly from others, then you need to start thinking about specific ways in which to demonstrate this part of your brand in daily communications, meetings and presentations. For example, can you come up with an innovative or different way of explaining a complex challenge or objective? Could you use a flip-chart in meetings to illustrate a suggested course of action?

The espresso effect

To help understand your core brand or your brand DNA, you need to explore your life history so far. Examine all the experiences you've had that have defined you in some way. To aid this process, picture an espresso machine – imagine all the coffee beans being poured in at the top with each representing a pivotal moment in your life. Think about these in particular:

- your first day at school, first job, etc;
- university or college experiences;
- something someone said to you when you were young;
- a challenging time;
- a significant decision;
- stories and anecdotes.

FIGURE 5.7   The espresso effect

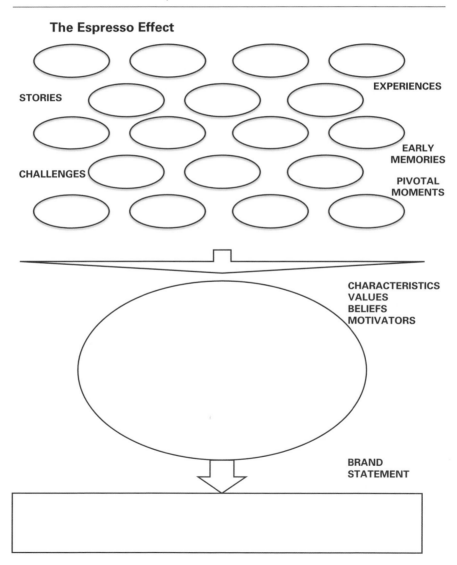

All of these coffee beans are ground and percolated to produce your values, talents, strengths, purpose, beliefs and drivers in life. In the condensed pure form in the espresso cup underneath are the few sentences that describe your authentic brand me, or your brand statement. This can form the basis of your LinkedIn profile for example. Even if you don't verbalize the content, it's important that you write it down and are clear about it in your mind.

Spend some time now to fill in the coffee beans and see what comes to mind. You will start to see that your life so far really has and continues to shape who you really are. You will start to see more clearly what you truly stand for and what is at your core. These stories and experiences will keep coming to you – try to keep a note of them all as they come to mind. These provide a great basis for presentations and adding authenticity, which we'll discuss more in Chapter 7, Presentational brand.

The middle box on the espresso effect model, Figure 5.7, is for your core values, characteristics, traits and strengths that you have now started to refine down from considering your brand this far. This is where the 'coffee beans' have been ground down to the really important and integral elements of your brand. This becomes your core essence. The final piece, the pure espresso in the cup underneath, represents your 'brand me' statement.

Brand me statement

From what we've covered in this chapter so far, you can start to form your brand me statement. Nobody wants to do business with somebody who is all things to all men, but rather with an expert in a field or discipline, or who is known for something very specific. Your statement is distinctive to you and you alone and you could liken it to a tagline or catchphrase. It is quite simply the short paragraph that specifically and uniquely describes you. You won't perfect it first time and it will evolve over time also. You may not verbalize it but the important thing is that you have clear in your mind what you stand for and how you want to be known.

Your brand me statement is one of the key components of your brand. You need it to give you a foundation to continually build your brand from. To be effective it needs to accurately portray your values, talents, purpose and passions, and your experience. It should sound like you and be easily recognizable as you to people who know you well. It must accurately describe who you are and who you aspire to be. It should answer what you are best at (your value), for whom (your audience) and how you do it uniquely (your USP – unique selling proposition).

Having a clear and solid brand me statement will help you to consistently communicate authentically.

I have covered more on the use of and enhancing your brand me statement in Chapter 6, Raising your visibility factor.

Here are a couple of examples of brand statements that will provide some thoughts and a basis for you and help you get started. Remember that every brand me statement is unique and personal and is also subjective, therefore the end result must feel right for you in both content and format. These are just guidelines.

Actual example:

- Jeffrey Hayzlett is a global business celebrity and former Fortune 100 c-suite executive. From small business to international corporations, he puts his creativity and extraordinary entrepreneurial skills into play, launching ventures blending his leadership perspectives, insights into professional development, mass marketing prowess and affinity for social media.

   This one could be further enhanced to include more about Jeffrey's personal values, but these arguably come across in his passions and skills.

Generic example:

- As a global retail business strategy expert, with 20+ years of international experience, I am driven by leading the successful amalgamation of cultures to create a strong and sustainable organization. I am particularly committed to ensuring a smooth transition for the people within a company and to creating a working environment that is highly positive, inspirational and empowering for every individual. It is important for me to help create and work within a culture that is truly aligned to putting our employees' happiness first, as I believe this will drive customer happiness as a result.

You can write this statement in the first or third person depending on where it will be used. The important thing is, however, that you have it crystallized in your mind. You will feel more in control of what your brand really is in a concise form, therefore will find it easier to project this when you're speaking, writing or being interviewed. Familiarize yourself with it even if you don't ever actually speak it out loud.

Your book title

You can add another dimension to your brand me statement by thinking about a relevant and unique title. Again it may be something you never actually verbalize, but it will help you to get closer to your true brand.

When I came up with the brand name Walking TALL for my business, it was as a result of having to create a book title for my first book. The publishers were pushing me for a title and in order to come up with something meaningful to me as a brand, I thought through my life history so far and considered the common threads. One thing that stuck out for me was the fact that I'm only 156 cm tall and I remembered being smaller than a lot of the other kids throughout my school years, which irritated me! Looking back, I worked hard at standing out from the crowd and thought of all the things I did to be more visible. Walking TALL then came to me as a result. This became the book title and subsequently I rebranded the company too. So if you were to consider your life history so far and write this into a book, what would the title of your book be? Can you visualize the cover? These elements will help you to bring your brand statement to life and ensure you have that deep personal element to it. Who knows, some of you may actually write that book too!

A while ago I was coaching a retail expert and consultant who specialized in mergers and acquisitions in the retail sector. As part of the programme we worked on her brand statement and title. We needed to delve into what it is she really does at grassroots level in order to do this. What emerged in her own words was that when she goes into M&A situations, there is often confusion, demotivation and uncertainty, in fact a high degree of chaos all around. What she has the ability to do is see a clear picture of what is needed to 'fix' the situation and bring about a level of positivity once again. Her 'book title' therefore simply became 'Creating vision out of chaos'. She had the cover designed and used this as a constant visual reminder of her brand.

'Celebrity' brand me

'What do you want to be "famous" for?'

So what is it you want people to say about you behind your back? What would you most like to be known for or 'famous' for? If you think about celebrities who have really made it to the A list, they pretty much always have a strong and clear personal brand and we think of the same things when we think of them. Of course we don't have to like these celebrities for them to be great examples of personal brands. These are the words that come to my mind when I think of these people:

- Oprah Winfrey – humanitarian, philanthropist, queen of talk show, influential
- Lady Gaga – flamboyant, diverse, dramatic, supreme performer, weird dresser
- David Beckham – dedication, respect for people, style, charisma, authentic
- Warren Buffet – investor, business magnate, frugality, philanthropist

What they all have in common is they are experts at branding themselves for something unique that makes them as marketable as possible in their field and in some cases to sponsors. They are all consistent at managing this brand, because it's authentic to them. They look at what it is they have that is most marketable and that will get them to where they want to be. Then they package that brand and project it powerfully and consistently. Those celebrities that drop off the edge with their brand are those that either had a brand that wasn't as consistent as it could be or that fell from a great height and monumentally uprooted the foundation of the brand they are known for – for example Tiger Woods. He managed to destroy the very basis of the brand we had been sold, that of innocence and a clean-cut Disney-like image. We felt cheated when the affair allegations became clear. In another example, actor Charlie Sheen may have destroyed his reputation with reports of his bad boy image; however, perhaps his character or brand as consistently portrayed by the media has lessened the surprise of the downfall of his brand in our eyes. Therefore, has it made him more marketable in some way because the brand image meets the expectation and is consistent? An arguable point.

Brands are fragile. It's important to recognize that negative perceptions are much more powerful than positive perceptions. It can take years to build a positive personal brand and this can be destroyed immediately by a negative event. Transparency and honesty are critical. Tiger's reluctance to speak about the situation was as much a problem as the issue itself. People wanted an acknowledgement and a degree of remorse. Failure to give this resulted in the Tiger brand becoming even more damaged.

When brands become damaged for the very reason they were made, the impact is even greater. Take Martha Stewart and Paula Deen – both prominent in the homemaking industry. Both experienced major and public turmoil over personal actions that threatened to destroy their massive success – Martha for tax evasion and Paula for trying to become the face of healthy living in order to promote a diabetes product and admitting she has Type 2 diabetes, after making her name with her high-fat and -sugar cooking. Martha went to jail but her brand suffered less. Why? Because Paula violated her brand promise and severely diluted the brand she was known for. Martha didn't.

A few years ago, I was working on an ITV documentary on the David Beckhan brand – of course arguably one of the most valuable personal brands in the world today. This programme was launched just after his alleged affair with his personal assistant in Spain. We carried out a survey as part of the programme – this showed us that 50 per cent of people blamed David Beckham for this alleged affair, and the other 50 per cent blamed his wife Victoria! Quite an incredible conclusion, but the reason for this was that it didn't fit with the Beckham brand that we think we all know, and that the media reinforce all the time. The Beckham brand is so consistent and strong that we don't quite believe it and therefore our view is: if this did happen it must have been somebody else's fault! I called it the 'Beckham blip' and spoke on BBC News about it. We can use this example to examine our own equivalents in terms of our consistent brand – what do you do so consistently well that when you don't quite deliver to expectations because things go a little off course, then it's considered a blip and not part of your brand? We can't be 100 per cent consistent but if we are constantly adding layers to our brand that reinforce who we really are, then when we have to dilute it at times, it doesn't make too much of an impact.

Whatever way we look at it, people will always have a few words that come to mind when they think of us, or have a collection of powerful and clear ideas in their mind. We just have to ensure that we manage those words and ideas as effectively as possible so they are in alignment with our authentic character and brand and not off-message. It is important to remember what Maya Angelou said: 'I've learned that people will forget what you said, people will forget what you did, but people will never forget how you made them feel.'

What are the few words you'd like others to think about when they think of you? If you are to truly manage your brand to its maximum, then you have to think like a celebrity and market yourself with this mindset.

Internal brand ambassadors

Personal brands can bring to life an organization's culture that no digital image, cutting-edge website or marketing brochure can. Large global companies are starting to tap into this aspect of branding more and more, and rather than see the personal branding exploits of their most prominent leaders as rebellious and self-promotional, they have now come to treat them as their company's most coveted brand ambassadors. The most successful companies help employees understand their personal brands and how they can reinforce the corporate brand via their own personal authenticity.

Consumers increasingly base their feelings about a company on what they know about its people, so encouraging the personal branding of your employee base – particularly your senior leaders – is critical. Coaching on presentation skills, for example, is no longer just related to internal company conferences and team meetings; it is often focused on enhancing the individual's ability to present to global corporate conferences outside of the business and even the industry sector. There are some great examples of corporate leaders becoming highly respected speakers outside of their company and even industry. We heard in Chapter 4 about how Andrew Grill from IBM views the importance of leaders with strong personal brands in their own right. Phil Jones, managing director of Brother UK, is another corporate leader with a great brand. He has become known as an accomplished speaker on future trends and leadership, and is respected by professional speakers worldwide. This level of speaking competence from a corporate leader is unusual. Phil believes that Brother UK's brand can be significantly enhanced with immense feelings of positivity due to the real stories that he and other leaders can bring. 'It shows some personality about who we are as a business. A business is a community of individuals and personalities. In order to attract the talent pipeline that we need as a business today, my external presence as a public speaker and digitally, helps to create the relevancy and social breadcrumb trail for this generation in particular.'

As we know, engaged employees are the most powerful brand asset you have. If you're not inspiring your talent to be brand ambassadors, then you are missing out on a huge opportunity to build authentic brand awareness. According to the 2013 Edelman Trusts Barometer, employees rank higher in the public trust factor than the company's PR department. Some 41 per cent of us believe that employees are the most credible source of information regarding the business. When a customer interacts with one of your front-line employees, everything your PR and marketing departments have created will be put to the test. In other words, it is the behaviours of your employees that give the strongest messages about your brand.

Building rapport and maintaining your brand

So having thought more about your brand, one of the challenges now is how you keep your brand intact and keep adding the positive reinforcing layers when you communicate and interact with others who have a different personality type to you. A tool we use in our programmes is called Clarity4D. There are many personality profiling tools on the market that are excellent. We choose to use this one as it works very well with the personal branding process to support key messages.

Clarity4D produces unique personal profiles using a behavioural model and psychometric tools based on the work of Carl Jung. The profiles identify four personality types that are linked to the four elements, identified by Aristotle, of fire, water, air and earth. The use of colour helps people to identify and remember the differences. The concept is that as individuals, we have all four colour 'energies' within us, and we are capable of using all four, but we may have a preference for using one or two with which we are most comfortable. It's a very simple tool to use and provides us with data that can effectively be mapped over the brand profile you have started to create for yourself to enable better and more practical use of the report. The full profile can be completed to identify your strengths and areas for potential growth – you can do this online at **www.walkingtall.org** and can contact **www.clarity4d.com** for some further information. Here are some ideas from it that can help you to adapt or modify your communication style to connect with the preferred way of interacting with others, in order to create rapport and develop effective relationships with others.

The four colour 'energies' with descriptions are:

- water – blue: reflective, observing, analytical, cautious, formal, exacting;
- fire – red: focused, forceful, direct, challenging, dominant, action-orientated;
- earth – green: empathic, concerned, informal, supportive, patient, easy-going;
- air – yellow: talkative, expressive, light-hearted, sociable, flamboyant, enthusiastic.

Decide which set of words most accurately describes you.

By looking at the above characteristics, we can clearly see how the different personality preferences could potentially clash at times. With greater

FIGURE 5.8 Clarity4D chart

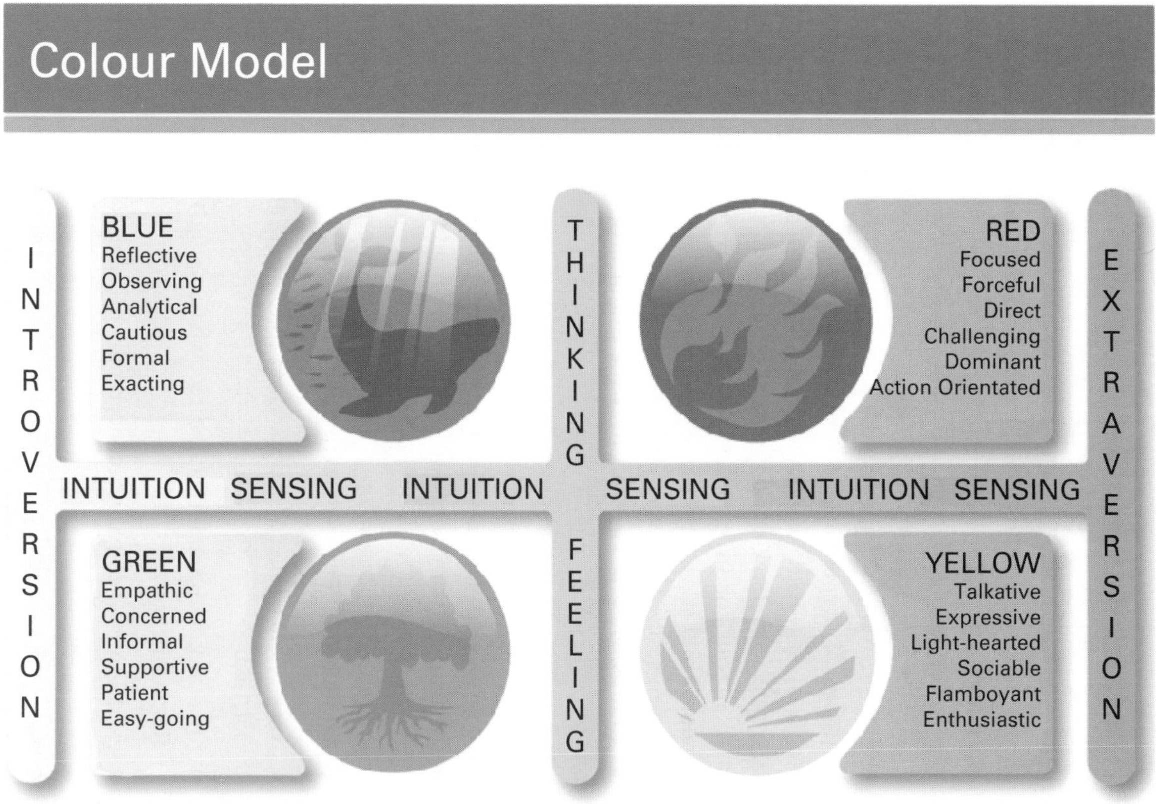

Colour Model

INTROVERSION

THINKING

BLUE
Reflective
Observing
Analytical
Cautious
Formal
Exacting

RED
Focused
Forceful
Direct
Challenging
Dominant
Action Orientated

EXTRAVERSION

INTUITION SENSING INTUITION SENSING INTUITION SENSING INTUITION SENSING

FEELING

GREEN
Empathic
Concerned
Informal
Supportive
Patient
Easy-going

YELLOW
Talkative
Expressive
Light-hearted
Sociable
Flamboyant
Enthusiastic

self-awareness and understanding of the different strengths of each colour energy type, it can help us as individuals to manage our personal brand, and participate more effectively within a team, with clients, and in our personal relationships, In order to manage our personal brand, we need to consider how best to communicate with each different personality type to achieve desired outcomes.

When speaking with someone with a preference for a colour 'energy' that is different from yours, here are some tips for effective communication:

Blue 'energy'

Do:

- respect his or her need for privacy;
- write details down for him or her;
- research details before a meeting with him or her.

Do not:

- push for an immediate answer;
- finish his or her sentences;
- indulge in social chit-chat.

Red 'energy'

Do:

- get straight to the point;
- take ownership of problems;
- keep up with his/her pace.

Do not:

- become emotional;
- appear negative or critical;
- waffle or procrastinate.

Green 'energy'

Do:

- allow time for him or her to feel comfortable;
- appreciate his or her loyalty;
- take time to talk to him or her personally.

Do not:

- appear insincere;
- push for a quick response;
- give insensitive feedback.

Yellow 'energy'

Do:

- adopt an informal manner;
- acknowledge his/her creative approach;
- offer a variety of tasks and topics.

Do not:

- impose restrictions and procedures;
- send long, detailed reports;
- ignore his/her need for some response.

Let's imagine a scenario in a typical corporate organization. There is a meeting of the executive team, and some important outcomes are needed:

Mr/Ms Red sees the big picture, has already made a decision and wants to take action immediately. Mr/Ms Blue is cautious and would like to have time to do some detailed research and analysis before making a decision. Mr/Ms Green considers the impact of the project on the team, and wants to spend time getting people on board before committing to anything. Mr/Ms Yellow hasn't done any preparation for the project yet because they like to come along to the meeting to discuss, be creative by brainstorming and do their thinking as they talk.

The dynamics of this team could potentially be very powerful if everyone recognizes and respects the strengths of each other, but without the understanding and ability to 'flex' their communication style, frustrations and misunderstandings could create a dysfunctional team.

Another typical scenario could be that the executive team is made up of several people with similar colour energies – typically red and blue – and the diversity and richness of people with different preferences is missing from the team, so all decisions could be made from a very analytical, process approach, and miss out on innovation, creativity and teamwork.

It is important for each member of the team to understand how and why their colleagues think and behave in the way they do. With that knowledge, greater understanding and cooperation can be developed, which will result in a more harmonious, efficient and effective team.

We all see things from our own perspective and subconsciously assume others see everything the same way as us. Stepping into each others' world and seeing things from a different viewpoint helps to build rapport.

These, of course, are just some guidelines – I would suggest that you and your teams explore this in more depth with the detailed reports.

Relationships and the extended Johari window

You are probably familiar with the Johari window technique in Figure 5.9.1, which was originally developed by two US psychologists, Joseph Luft (1916–2014) and Harrington Ingham (1914–95). It was developed to help people better understand their relationship with themselves and others.

In Figure 5.9.2 we have provided (courtesy of Rachel Cowan, Walking TALL trainer and coach) an extended view of the Johari window to illustrate

FIGURE 5.9.1   The Johari window

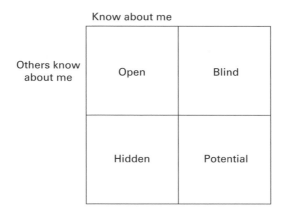

FIGURE 5.9.2   The extended concept

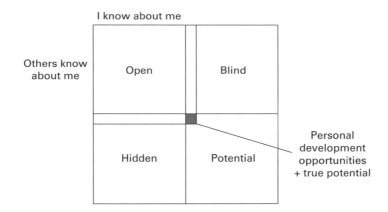

how you can enhance your personal development and build more rapport by being more open about yourself.

The top left quadrant is called the open window. It is the parts of you that are known to you, which you are open to revealing and discussing with others. The bottom left is the hidden window, the parts that you know about yourself but others don't.

The top right quadrant, are your blind spots or the parts of you that others see and you don't. The bottom left quadrant is your hidden potential.

Given that we can only work with what we know about ourselves, the only way we can tap into our potential is choose to be more vulnerable and disclose parts of us that are normally hidden. What will then happen is others will start to give you more feedback and give you more information about yourself that you didn't know, so the hidden and blind spot quadrants are extended. Only then can you tap into your true potential.

So the key is to find people you trust and put yourself into a situation that stretches you, give more hidden information about yourself in a safe environment then you will get more from others.

Furthermore, the whole windowpane is always the same size. However, the individual quadrants can change in size.

Imagine now two Johari windows.

The window on the right in Figure 5.9.3 is yours, and the one on the left is your colleague's, which has been flipped to mirror yours. The relationship between the two people can only be as big as the biggest quadrant.

If your colleague is only prepared to have this much open, this is the limit to how far the relationship can go. If you find that somebody is closing you down it is important that you analyse the situation effectively. For instance some people may be shutting you down because they don't like the depth of the topic that you are discussing. You may be comfortable with this level of vulnerability; however, the other person may not. Therefore their 'open' window may be smaller than yours, for this particular discussion point. Even though we don't know what they are, there are very good reasons that this person does not want to discuss this topic at the level of vulnerability that you do. To preserve the relationship you must pull back on the discussion

FIGURE 5.9.3   Rapport limitations

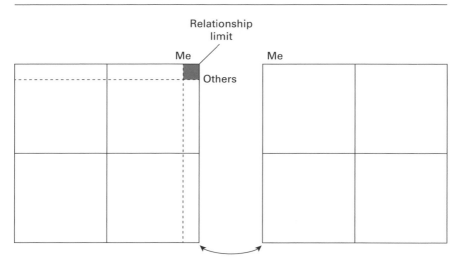

and bring it back to a more superficial level or switch topics. If possible try not to end the conversation at this point as you are leaving the other person in an uncomfortable place, which may affect your relationship going forward. Encourage, affirm and make it clear that you like the person and agree with the parts that you feel comfortable with. This will create trust with the person, which leaves the opportunity for their open window to become larger the next time you engage with them.

There are times when we all display a small open window. These are the situations when we feel anxious, afraid or uncomfortable. The size of our open window in different situations is an important factor to track. If we feel ourselves closing our open window we should ask our self 'what am I afraid of?' If we are afraid of finding out a truth about ourselves with a close friend or 'safe colleague' perhaps we should consider opening our window slightly to be willing to hear and address the feedback. It is these situations that help us reach our potential and continue to grow.

Both the Clarity4D and Johari window concepts are crucial for maintaining a strong personal brand when we communicate directly with others.

Rolling out a brand training experience

In my experience, most run-of-the-mill customer-service programmes, 'live the values' posters or 'brand immersion' sessions rarely get to the level required to enable individuals to internalize and interpret the corporate values in order to change behaviours. This is because the programmes provided often fall short of addressing the 'what's in it for me' factor that is needed today for employees to feel they want to learn, change and develop. Contrary to management beliefs, having a brand new glossy corporate image is not enough to excite and motivate them and move them to truly 'living the brand'. We have to go a stage deeper to achieve this and that is getting to the heart of the individual and what drives them. What's needed is a brand training *experience* that is about them as an individual.

This is where you can link personal brand to corporate brand. Take your employees out of the corporate space for a period of time, and get them to focus on themselves and on being the best they can be authentically. This will allow them to focus on what's important to them and inspire them to fully engage with the corporate values and the behaviours that will not only aid their career development but achieve corporate brand objectives too.

Different communities in your business will require a tailored approach for this training experience; however, the content and process will be similar.

It's the delivery type, language and pace that need to be tailored in order to ensure full buy-in. In my experience, the content of personal branding programmes is embraced easily by all levels if tailored in this way due to the personal nature of the content. A buzz is created around the company as people go through the programme, and an organic lift in positivity, feedback and self-awareness is often reported. This result is created of course when the 'what's in it for me' factor is appropriately met.

Keeping momentum

With a focus in many organizations on the 70-20-10 rule now – 70 per cent on-the-job learning, 20 per cent learning from others/managers and 10 per cent formal training, any learning experience needs to be focused, practical and easily implemented into everyday interactions.

Gone are the days of a 'one dip' approach to training – today we need to use innovative ways in which to keep employees engaged and keep momentum with the key principles alive and thriving. As well as your leaders, Generation Y coming into your organization will demand that training is fast-paced, agile and relevant and will value the importance placed on it being worthwhile and time well spent in their important and busy schedules.

I would suggest you consider a combination of ways in which to engage employees with a personality of the brand programme and of course your learning and development department can advise on this. This blended learning flow is often the thread for our programmes (see Figure 5.10 on page 137).

Creating a reward or recognition scheme that recognizes staff behaviours that embody the essence of the corporate values and help create the desired culture is an effective way to keep the messages alive. Encourage your teams to develop their own model for rewarding great team behaviours and create a feedback culture for keeping each other on track.

So in this chapter we have come some way to defining your personal brand and have explored the following:

- the basics of defining your personal brand;
- determining your values;
- gaining feedback;
- mapping that feedback over your brand profile;
- modifying behaviours when communicating with other personality types;
- defining where the development gaps are for action.

FIGURE 5.10   Blended learning flow

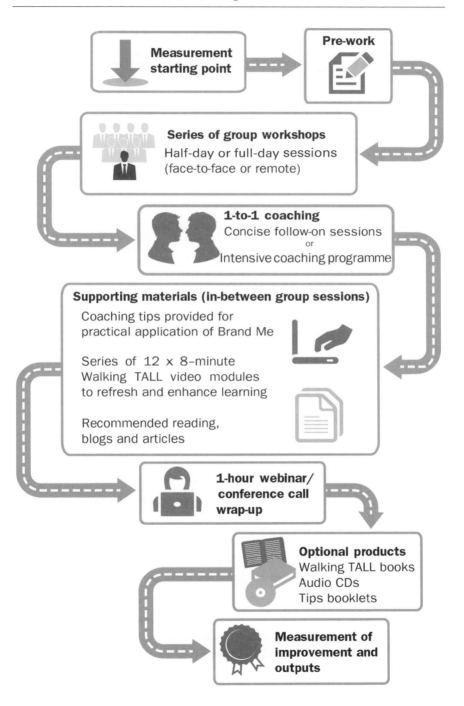

FIGURE 5.11   Brand me map

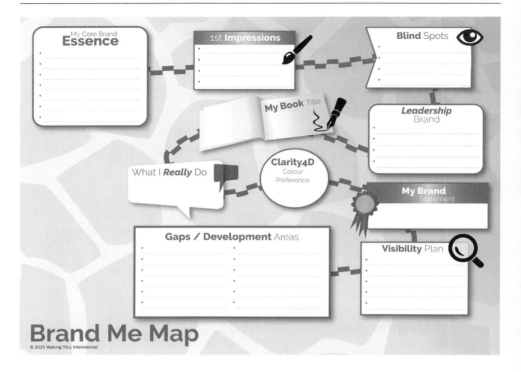

At this point, you can start to complete your brand me map – see Figure 5.11. It will keep you on track with your brand development as it evolves over time.

Each element of your brand me map explained:

- Your core brand essence – the descriptive words you have filtered down from the exercises so far and in particular the espresso effect. These are the words that truly embody who you are.

- First impressions – any feedback you have gathered that relates to the initial impression you have made on others. This is not easy to get so always be on the lookout for opportunities to extract it from people.

- Blind spots – when gathering your feedback you will have been provided with some things that you were not aware of about yourself, both good and not so good. Record these here so you are more consciously aware of them to work on or capitalize on.

- Book title – the title of your book if you were to write your life history so far. This can become the title of your brand statement.

- Leadership brand – what are the words that you most want people to use to describe you as a leader behind your back? This will tell you much about the legacy you'd like to leave.

- What I really do – this is covered in Chapter 6 and it helps to ascertain what it is you really bring to the table as a unique brand.

- Clarity4D colour preference – record this here. If you've not been able to work yours out from the descriptions in this chapter, then go to our website and request completion of a profile from there.

- My brand statement – the final result of the work done on your brand me statement.

- Gaps/development areas – the danger zones for you that have transpired from the feedback you have received and/or the areas you have highlighted for yourself as needing more focus.

- Visibility plan – this is covered in Chapter 6 and will help you to create a strategy for building more personal brand exposure.

Of course, this content will keep evolving over time so it's fine to create a newly tweaked one every few months. Keep your brand me map visible so that every day your personal brand development is in your conscious mind.

Remember, your personal brand is unique to you, it cannot be copied and it is your own 'intellectual property'. Treat it as such and ensure that you value it, nurture it, develop it to position you where you want to be in order to be perceived in the authentic way you deserve to be perceived.

References

Edelman (2013) [accessed on 11 October 2015] '2013 Edelman Trust Barometer' [Online] www.edelman.com/insights/intellectual-property/trust-2013
Godin, S (2005) *The Purple Cow: Transform your business by being remarkable*, Penguin, London

Raising your visibility factor

06

Gone are the days when it was perfectly acceptable for the CEO and the senior leadership team to operate only out of their executive offices, not to be seen on a regular basis and to leave all the public events to their colleagues in PR and communications. Does this sound like you?

This chapter will look at the necessity for increased visibility today for business leaders, how to measure where you're at right now and then how to go about creating the plan and putting it into action. There are many ways of raising visibility and it's not all about shouting from the rooftops about who you are and what you've achieved, those introverts among you will be pleased to know!

We'll be covering:

- what visibility means in the business world;
- measuring where you're at now with your visibility factor;
- creating your visibility plan;
- gaining clarity on what you really bring to the table;
- enhancing your brand me statement;
- your digital brand;
- effective networking and building your network;
- managing your brand in the media.

As we've seen in Chapter 4, CEO reputation is a fundamental driver of corporate reputation and its contribution to market value is now showing as 44 per cent according to research by Weber Shandwick (2015). There is no expectation of this reducing either; in fact it is expected to increase. In addition, global executives attribute 45 per cent of their company's reputation to the reputation of their CEO. As top visibility coach David Avrin says, 'It's not who you know, it's who knows you that counts.'

Corporate executives attribute 45 per cent of company reputation to the reputation of their CEO

It is equally important for the senior leadership team to be aware of their impact on company brand reputation. Whoever the stakeholder, they don't really care if it's the CEO, the chief finance officer or the head of corporate communications who says or does the right or wrong thing. They are all seen as the personality of the company brand in equal measures and they will all have a similar impact on the corporate reputation.

Visibility of the senior leadership team generally tends to be limited to a crisis situation or an announcement of financial results; in other words, it tends to be reactive. Times have changed and now it's necessary for business leaders to be proactive about their exposure and visibility and manage it in line with building the reputation of the company and other brand awareness efforts. It presents a significant opportunity for your company to stand out and embrace the freedom you now have in various forms to increase exposure in strategic ways.

There is a need today not just to raise your personal profile through more exposure and management of your personal brand internally and externally, but also for adding that crucial level of personality to your organization and allowing your clients (current and potential) and all other stakeholders to feel a connection to the brand through your brand as a leader and ambassador.

Let's now focus on how you can achieve this increased level of visibility and exposure. Of course, these techniques can and should be deployed across all levels of management, and talent and high-performance communities too. As Eleri Sampson referenced in her book *Build Your Personal Brand*, the three biggest factors in career progression are:

- 10 per cent – doing your job;
- 30 per cent – attitude and behaviour;
- 60 per cent – visibility and exposure (Sampson, 2002).

60 per cent of career progression is down to visibility and exposure

Therefore, these techniques for raising your visibility and profile are applicable to anybody wanting to enhance their career and build their personal brand.

FIGURE 6.1 The personal brand visibility layer

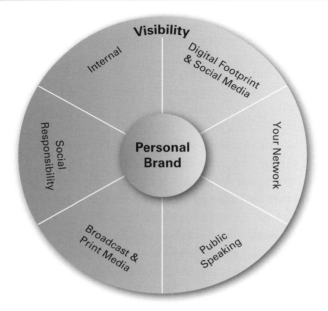

First, I would suggest you gain some feedback and assess yourself in your current level of visibility, internally and externally. Use this feedback checklist with your senior team, your middle managers and a selection of employees from different areas and levels. You should also complete the checklist yourself and see how your scores come out differently to the feedback you get. This will tell you a lot about the gaps in the perception of your visibility levels.

Level of visibility

1 = Weak   5 = Strong

1 participation in external networking events;

2 appearance at internal events;

3 contributions to print media;

4 seen and heard on broadcast media;

5 presentations at public events;

6 well-known in the industry;

7 social media presence;

8 general visibility among employee base;

9 public awareness;

10 level of increase in visibility in last three years.

Total up your average score

- 40+ – You're doing a pretty good job already with your visibility and exposure. What do you do best that you can capitalize on and what are the small elements that can still be improved upon?

- 30–39 – Not bad; however, there are some areas you need to improve on. Highlight what these are and make sure you build them into your personal development plan. Work these through with your coach if you have one. By the way, if you don't have a coach at the senior level at which you work, I would strongly urge you to seek one. You need this perspective on your brand.

- 20–29 – Visibility is not your strong area and you possibly need some guidance on how best to improve this in a way that works for you. You probably try some things but don't necessarily look for the opportunities to increase visibility enough. This is a strong area of development for you.

- 10–19 – Definitely a weakness for you. You probably avoid networking, public events, the media and social media at all costs and don't feel comfortable in that space. Work with a coach to help you to develop the confidence in these areas – it's not something you can avoid any longer.

Having gathered this feedback you will have a better idea of where you are on the visibility scale right now and can start to see where the effort needs to go to raise your visibility factor.

There are really three main areas of visibility for you as a senior leader to consider: your internal stakeholders (employees, rest of the leadership team and non-executive directors), your external stakeholders (investors, analysts, clients and customers, partners, suppliers) and the rest of the world (the general public, potential clients, influencers of your brand, the media, other industry leaders, generations of tomorrow etc). All need to be considered when building your visibility plan as they are each important factors to building a strong reputation and enhancing your employer brand.

We have to recognize that increasing your visibility and exposure comes with potential hazards too. However, this is not a strong enough reason to avoid doing it. Therefore, it does need careful planning to ensure alignment with your personal brand as a senior leader and your company brand. I would suggest that your head of corporate communications be involved in the visibility strategy process for you and your leadership team, to give an objective perspective and aid consistency.

Be clear what you're aiming for

Before you start creating your visibility strategy you need to be clear about what it is you want to achieve from a corporate perspective, and what brand messages you want to consistently project. Refer back to Chapter 5 where you spent time thinking about your unique authentic brand and always have this right at the forefront of your mind when putting the strategy together.

A good coaching technique for setting objectives is to use this structure:

I want to... [set out the objective]

By... [a specific date, for example 30 June (in two years' time)]

So that I... [what does this give you personally when you achieve it?]

The last piece is the most important as this is the part that will hold you personally accountable to reaching the objective. You need to be clear about what this gives you personally when it's achieved. Unless you fulfil a personal need then you are less likely to really engage with the objective and therefore achieve it. So even if the goal is to become a top 100 employer, there needs to be a win for you too. Perhaps it's personal pride, satisfaction, fulfilment etc? Do work on getting to the core of what this gives you and you'll find it a lot easier to achieve the goal.

Of course, your goal may be entirely to raise your visibility level. If so, still think about why, what it gives you when you achieve it and how you're going to measure your success.

It also allows the brain to focus on a specific event, such that the brain becomes a magnet for attracting and spotting the opportunities to move you nearer to the goal. Without this focus, you can easily miss world-class moments to capitalize on.

Getting started

Create a list of people who will help you achieve this goal or can influence it in some way. Ask yourself who needs to know who you are and what you're great at. Some ideas:

- industry journalists and media contacts;
- content writers, experts and bloggers in your industry;
- authors who could reference you in their books and articles;
- events organizers for relevant conferences (industry-specific or otherwise);

- your very own head of communications and the communications team;
- your counterparts in the industry;
- your counterparts in other industry areas;
- prominent people in the community;
- CEOs of local or major charities;
- organizers of charity dinners and events;
- local celebrities who are in alignment with the corporate brand;
- non-executive director agency owners.

There will be others that you will add to this list as you work with it. Just engaging your brain with the thinking will create ideas for you. Your head of communications should be able to add strategically to the list too.

How are you doing it?

Now you need to work on how you are going to be more visible with these people. Being visible is not always about being face-to-face visible. A great example I had of this was a few years ago in Singapore, where I was speaking at a conference. I met several people there of course, and most I forgot about a few months later. I had a short conversation on branding with one particular guy there that I also forgot about a couple of months down the line. Four months after the event I had a package arrive in the mail from Singapore, from the same guy. There was a nicely branded card with a note to me personally, and some newspaper cuttings in the envelope. The message read along the lines of 'Dear Lesley, I saw these in the newspaper the other day and thought they might be of interest to you.' They were – two articles on branding and one on a baby giraffe that had been born in Singapore Zoo. He had remembered my business and also that my brand centres on a giraffe. I felt good because it was about me and he was not trying to sell me anything. However, his business is about strategic planning for small businesses so guess where I'm going to go when I need that service in my business. He keeps himself visible and on my radar every few months with similar mailings, so he's in my mind for when the time is right.

Often we assume we are at the forefront of people's minds when that next opportunity crops up, as we're the obvious choice or it's our turn, but the reality is we're not necessarily on their radar, unless we proactively manage our visibility.

Here are some thoughts and ideas for how you might build your visibility. Work out what is most appropriate for each person on your plan.

- Make yourself easily contactable and available to the media – broadcast, online and print media. There are websites such as expertsources.co.uk where journalists can easily find you related to particular topics and keywords.

- Contribute articles to magazines in your industry. Consider publications outside of your industry too, where appropriate.

- Comment on specific topics in blogs and articles online.

- Have a regular presence on your internal intranet.

- Make sure your photo and a profile piece is on your company website The rest of the leadership team should be there too. Executive team details without photos are always impersonal. Ensure they are professionally taken though and consistent in style.

- Forward relevant and interesting articles to people on your visibility list – either electronically or through the mail. Sometimes mailing it makes a refreshing change and it gets noticed more.

- Is there a successful corporate initiative you could have written up or be interviewed on that the industry or wider business audience could be interested in?

- Work with your head of communications to create a profile sheet on you for forwarding to relevant media sources. This could generate profile interviews and speaking opportunities.

- Make contact with event organizers who need speakers for industry events. Devise a mechanism that works for you to keep personal notes about people. For example, when you met that person at the awards dinner and they mentioned going on a holiday of a lifetime the following week – make a note to follow up and see how it went. People love you to be interested in them; it makes you a more interesting person.

- Commit to speaking at three charity or local community events in the next six months.

- Build into your daysome walkabouts with a purpose, around your office, stores or branches and meet a few new employees every week. Make sure the conversation you engage in is more about them though.

- Create a system to remember names – use of a visual image that comes to mind instantly when you meet them helps.

- Thank people for a job well done, a positive contribution to the brand, their support, for example, either publicly or by a simple thank you card that they will remember. Touchnote.com or the App is fantastic for taking a photo and sending as a postcard or card to somebody.

- Follow up promptly with people you met at an event – avoid e-mail and find another suitable way. Try Eyejot, for example – a short video e-mail tool that creates a visual connection.

- Connect people to people where appropriate – this is always appreciated and remembered.

- Have your assistant work on or filter suitable targeted events for you to attend. Send a relevant book.

- Make sure you are visible on social media, but in an appropriate way. There will be more on this below.

Working through these will enable you to engage with the process and you will find yourself more aware of the opportunities to be visible and memorable as they crop up.

A word of warning here and it's a bit of a paradox, but always ensure that you have a degree of humility, or make it about the other person, when you are raising visibility. As a senior leader this is always appreciated and is conducive to your likeability and authenticity and overall impact.

Being interested in others

Will Kintish is a good friend of mine and is an expert on networking. He coined the phrase 'Being interested in others makes you a more interesting person'. I totally agree and it's a conscious thought I keep in my mind. People love it when you remember things about them and refer to it. For example, that client who was about to embark on a big adventure last time you saw them and you remember to mention it next time. Or with Julie in accounts, when her son Jonny broke his leg playing football last week and you remember to check in with her to see how he is. These things go a million miles to making you memorable and impactful. Of course, it needs to be done sincerely and authentically too.

I will always be reminded of how powerful this can be from an experience I had a few years ago. I was starting a coaching programme for a company secretary of a FTSE 100 company, so a very busy man with an international role. During the small talk at the beginning of the first session, we were talking about my son Max, who had just got his place at Cardiff University but not yet sorted out his accommodation with two weeks to go. I saw this client for his second session about eight weeks later. The very first thing he asked me was 'How did Max get on? Did he sort out his accommodation at Cardiff?' I was totally amazed that this busy man remembered something of no consequence to him, and the details also. Of course, he has left a very positive impression on me and will be remembered and talked about because of it.

Be interested in others to be remembered

Conversely, literally as I'm writing this chapter, I'm sitting in a little coffee shop in Pacific Grove in California. I cannot help but overhear a conversation between a man and a woman on the table next to me, who have obviously just met for the first time on a casual date. After around 25 minutes of hearing all about him, his successes, his business, his life, he says out of the blue 'So now tell me about you.' I was waiting for the extra bit: 'Tell me what you think about me.' The poor lady was given around two minutes, uninterrupted, to talk about herself, but with no active listening going on or comments about what she said. Then he cut in again with stories about him. After about 10 more minutes of this, the inevitable happened and the lady quickly said she had to go, said goodbye and made a speedy departure. He went back to his phone, apparently completely oblivious to what impact he had had.

Asking questions about others and active listening by asking questions back is attractive and compelling. The scenario described above is the exact opposite.

I know your life is very busy and it's often not easy to build in this extra activity and way of thinking. However, try it for a week and you'll start to see how the brain will begin to spot the opportunities to do this more, without you having to think about it consciously.

What I really do

When you're absorbed in the running of the business, managing people, answering to stakeholders, firefighting, responding to the next challenge, it's understandable that you have little time to really think about your brand and what it is you really do for the company. However, before you start to build visibility in force, you really need to spend time on defining this. Working with your team will help this process as others can often see it more clearly than you can.

You will have heard of the elevator pitch I'm sure – the process by which you define who you are and what you do in a few words, in a succinct, meaningful and marketable way. The process we're going to use here goes a little deeper than that and will lead to you compiling an effective brand statement.

Use this structure to dig down to the roots of what you really bring to the table:

> Well, my title is [CEO of ACME Building Supplies], but I like to think what I actually do for the company is... And the output is...

Or:

> You know how [the finance industry struggles to...] and as a result it causes [this to happen...]. Well, what I do is... And consequently...

You need to go deeper than operational areas alone and examine what you and your brand actually bring to this end result. What gives you the right to hold this position; what collective traits, attitudes, skills and experiences do you uniquely possess that enable you to carry out this role as effectively as you do? How do you do this job differently to anybody else because of who you are and your life experiences?

Some words you could add in here to help draw out the pertinent content are:

> I'm able to do this effectively because...
> I have an ability to...
> I have a passion for...
> I have strong values of [...] that drive me to...

Refer back to the thinking you did in Chapter 5 around your brand, as there will be lots of areas to bring in from there too.

If you consider how you would answer constant questions from a 10-year-old child who wants to understand what you do, why and how, this will help to bring out the details you need.

I often recommend to my clients that they should speak to schoolchildren in the community wherever possible. This will really get you thinking about what your job entails and why you're great at it, to a level of clarity that you don't often consider. It will also put you out of your comfort zone, give you a new experience and ultimately be rewarding too. In addition, school events are often covered in the local media and appear online too, so are great for your exposure. This is a 'must' consideration for your visibility plan, so look now for the opportunities to organize it.

Enhancing your brand statement

When you have clarified what it is you really do, verbalize it to a few others who know you and your role well. They will be able to help you refine it even more and it'll start to take real shape. The next stage is to condense it into a succinct and compelling paragraph that would be suitable for a profile sheet, short biography or LinkedIn summary. If you're going to be consistent with the brand you want to project you need to work on this and pin it down to something you are comfortable with and that is easily understood and remembered by others. It will and should of course evolve over time as your goals change and your motivators shift focus. In Chapter 5 we covered creating your brand me statement. This can be added to with the content discussed here to create a fully rounded statement of your brand.

Your digital personal brand

Having established that your brand as CEO or a senior leader is closely connected with the brand of the company as seen by others, the way in which your brand is portrayed in the digital world is a powerful opportunity to grow the corporate brand and create a fan base bigger than was ever possible before social media. It gives you an opportunity to build credibility, as you will be seen to put yourself out there embracing the digital world, thereby building even more trust and loyalty than has been possible in previous years. Business leaders have entered a virtual age of opportunity to tell their stories, share their biographies and echo their future strategies. CEOs are now placed in the spotlight for good or bad and this digital medium for portraying your brand and that of your company should be fully embraced.

In today's business world people want to do business with other people more so than ever before. However, we feel a stronger need to trust people generally, and we trust people we know and who we have relationships with. That's why it's important for you to build your personal brand and to reach as many people as possible with social media and create a solid digital footprint.

When did you last Google yourself? You should be doing this regularly to keep on top of how you are portrayed digitally. You can't ignore the fact that today if you don't show up online, then in the eyes of the searcher you quite simply do not exist! Executive recruitment firms verify this for me consistently. Many of them will Google you before they even look at your résumé. When you Google yourself look at the image results too to make sure there aren't any you don't want seen. It's not easy to delete these, but at least you can be aware of them.

Toby Turner, managing director of the London firm Holtby Turner Executive Search, says: 'We look for intelligent social awareness and contribution when assessing candidates from LinkedIn. We look for a profile that is up to date and consistently written, which shows attention to detail. Their engagement should be one of information giving, analysis as an influencer and with personal posts. Overall, it should be seen as helpful, open and sincere.'

The only way some people see you as a brand today is in the digital world. In the eyes of some people, for example Generation Y and Generation Z may dismiss you if they cannot find information about you on their search engines. Phil Jones, managing director at Brother UK, told me, 'I have on-boarding coffees with every new employee and I'm always amazed at how often they tell me they've done a full research job on me – they've read my blogs, Twitter feeds, LinkedIn profile as they want to understand me and the sort of person I am, the digital footprint I leave and therefore an insight into the culture at Brother UK.' So you can see that at the level you operate at you simply have to have an online or digital brand to positively serve the employer brand as well as your own personal brand.

There are of course several platforms you can use to expose your digital brand. However, you do need to make sure this is managed strategically. The three main ones for you to consider are:

- LinkedIn;
- Blogging;
- Twitter.

All have their advantages and disadvantages, so plan carefully how you use them. Here are some key tips for usage of the main ones in order to build and protect your brand.

LinkedIn is really considered the professional social media tool. As the chief evangelist at Canva and former Apple chief evangelist Guy Kawasaki says: 'The most important thing to remember is that unlike other social media sites where stupidity and silliness may be forgiven if not downright condoned, LinkedIn is all about your personal brand' (Carson, 2014).

LinkedIn is relationship-driven, and therefore is an individual one-to-one vetting system for people you'll do business with. Recommendations from peers, those you've line-managed and how generously someone gives kind words about you in their recommendations speaks volumes about how much of a team player and effective leader you actually are.

I would agree with the executive search firms that the absence of a LinkedIn profile could be extremely detrimental for your personal brand and profile generally, even if you're not looking for a new role. You may not be taken seriously if you're missing from online searches and LinkedIn will always be towards the top of most. LinkedIn is the place where people expect to find you. Be aware of how often you use Google searches for looking up somebody internally and externally, in order to glean something about them and an insight into their personality and interests. Be conscious that similar searches are happening on you, every day, from inside the company and outside.

As Toby Turner adds, 'LinkedIn has long moved on from "just the place where you set up a half hearted résumé". It should be seen as the "office sofa area" – a place where professionals gather and talk about business in an astute, friendly and open minded manner, respecting professional differences and seeing opportunity for personal development from the wealth of new associates.'

Key usage tips for ensuring a good LinkedIn profile:

- **Have a complete profile**
  Each area of the LinkedIn profile gives you a chance to show a little more about you as a professional person and your personal brand. Make sure you complete as many of the relevant ones as possible with this in mind, to maximize your digital profile.

- **Summary**
  This must be there, be well written and provide some authentic content about you, without bragging and using too much generic language. The summary is your opportunity to give a glimpse of your true personality, so make sure the wording uniquely describes you and is not such that it could be describing anybody. Use your brand me statement as a basis for this. Think about these areas:

  - Who do you want to reach with your LinkedIn profile? Make use of keywords in your heading. For example, people don't search for 'Director at xyz company' – that tells them nothing about you – they will search for 'marketing specialist' or in maybe my case 'personal branding coach'.

- What do you want people to feel about you when they read your summary?
- What are your most important accomplishments?
- What are your values, drivers and passions?

Here are a couple of examples.

How not to do it:

> A dynamic, self-motivated professional leader with the ability to drive change, and with a proven track record of high sales performance in various areas. Highly organized individual, believes in teamwork and motivating people, is highly effective at communicating, is agile, a blue-sky thinker and results-oriented.

Why doesn't this work? It's all subjective, the person's own view of themselves, but without being backed up by actual proof and examples of why this all might be true. It could also be describing anybody because of this.

A better version would be:

> I'm very driven to achieving significant goals with effective teamwork and by empowering others to reach their full potential. From 2010 to 2015, we exceeded annual sales targets in the team by increasing 15 per cent year on year. I'm at my best when I'm able to inspire the team by demonstrating value of their input to a project, providing the necessary support to enable the vision to be clarified and reached, and generally motivating them to have fun in their role as well as achieve. The last four quarters have seen us bring in an average of 26 per cent increase in sales over the same period last year, but most importantly have led to the comments from my team of 'What a fun, inspiring team this is to work in', 'We love it here – our views are listened to and we are valued for what we bring. This is leadership at its best.'

This kind of content provides some real-life proof of who you are and what you do best. Your profile will include very different information to that used here, of course. However, this will give you some idea of the overall style that you might want to use. It is a personal statement, so make it just that.

- Up-to-date photo
  Again this must be there (others think you are hiding something if it's not), and it needs to be a professional, close-up, head and shoulders shot. The visual first impression as we know gets remembered so this will have an impact on the perception others have of you before they meet you.

- Be active in discussions
  Build your profile and brand in this way but make sure your comments are appropriate and something that you would happily say to a journalist. Every post you make is a layer added to your personal brand.

- Not an online résumé
  Your LinkedIn profile is not intended to be an online résumé. Try not to include a long list of previous roles – the last three roles or companies are usually enough.

- Unsolicited invites to connect
  As a general rule, do not accept invites to connect from people that you have not met before or don't know of personally. I suggest sending a polite message back to ask where you might have met and that you have a policy of not connecting on LinkedIn with people you've not met before. If people can't be bothered to send a message to say this, then they are probably not worth connecting with. Remember, who you connect with is also a layer added to your personal brand.

  With the above point in mind, never send a connection to somebody without adding a personal message to introduce yourself. It's so much more impactful for your brand if you do this, and it gets remembered.

- Enhance your profile
  Add articles that you've written on LinkedIn's Pulse, which is LinkedIn's own blogging area. Also link to articles you have written elsewhere for magazines or other sites. Attach videos of you presenting or on panels, for example. This helps to position you as the brand you want to be 'famous' for.

  A recent update allows you to add a header image to your profile – it gives an instant visual summary of who you are and what your personal brand is.

  Add testimonials for your work that demonstrate and reinforce your brand as you want it to be seen.

As your profile photo is so crucial to your effective visibility and brand wherever it is used, here are a few added image wreckers to avoid:

- a picture of you standing next to a celebrity;

- you and someone who isn't famous;

- a photo of your dog;

- a company logo or any other logo (social media is personal);
- a picture of you from 100 yards away;
- a picture of you from 10 years ago;
- a group of people – which one is you?

If you look completely different on your profile photo from how you do in person, people will lose trust in you and you'll come across as unauthentic. Keep it real!

Toby Turner also added, 'Your Personal Brand value is a career currency and is driven by how valuable you are perceived in your professional network. We look for intelligent social awareness and contribution when assessing candidates from LinkedIn. Whether the profile is up to date and consistently written shows attention to details; their engagement should be one of information giving'.

If you're not entirely comfortable with using LinkedIn or any social media platform, there are many online courses available or perhaps book yourself on a half-day practical classroom programme. It'll be time very well spent – make it an action if necessary.

Sharing your thoughts and opinions via a blog

Blogging is a good way to raise your profile online and establish your brand. Writing regular articles that are relevant and related to what you want to be known for is a sure way to position yourself and your brand for exposure within your target market. Blogger.com is one of the most popular and easy to use, and as it is Google's free blogging tool, posts you publish here will rank well in Google.

Top tips for blogging

- Make it regular – if you can only add a post once per month that's ok, but if you can do one weekly it's even better. However, intermittent posts with long gaps between them won't really build your profile and may give a negative impression.
- A blog post needn't be long – in fact for more views you are better to keep them concise so people can read them quickly.

- Think about what you want to be known for and decide on some keywords that you want people to find you with. Make sure you add those keywords to your blog posts but do it in a natural way and if possible include one in your post title. Over time and with consistency you will move up the Google rankings for your chosen keywords.

- Only use professional quality images and make sure you have the right to use any images you do post.

Tweeting

Twitter is really a micro blog with only 140 characters per post, so it is limited in terms of content. However, providing links to your articles, blogs and other relevant content that support your brand is another great way to establish a good online presence.

We see several senior leaders of large organizations now tweeting regularly. Phil Jones, managing director of Brother UK and Andrew Grill, global managing partner at IBM Social Consulting, are two of those and I've mentioned them already regarding their strong personal brands. Phil Jones says that his visibility serves to enhance the brand of Brother UK. It creates comments such as, 'Oh yeah, I like Brother. I saw the CEO speak, and I follow him on Twitter'. Phil says that, 'It's important to be in the community that you serve – having proximity and relevance to the audience you are attracting.'

Twitter tips

- Add a profile picture – like LinkedIn this is essential.

- Add your keywords to your twitter profile so when people are searching for those terms you come up in their search.

- Twitter is less formal than LinkedIn, but remember although you can delete a tweet it may already have been seen by your followers, so don't tweet anything that could damage your brand or that of your company.

- Don't make your tweeting one way only. You should share your own blog posts and comments but make sure you regularly intersperse them with other people's content by tweeting it out to your followers. Retweet others' tweets and say thank you or return the favour when they Retweet yours.

- Twitter is a great way to get 'in the back door' when you want to connect or network with someone you haven't been able to contact by phone or meet in person. Start by following them and commenting on their tweets. This will often open an avenue for you to connect offline.

- Don't attempt to sell on Twitter – treat it as a way to meet and network with people or you may find your followers dwindling.

Other social networks to consider

- YouTube – being owned by Google, YouTube videos rank well in searches and it's the second-largest search engine after Google. If you have any videos of yourself presenting or discussing your company, products or services create a YouTube channel and upload them.

- Facebook – Although Facebook is considered more relaxed than LinkedIn and Twitter, and often just used for pure social use with friends, there is no denying that it has the biggest reach. So before you discount it, consider that most businesses will have a Facebook page and again it is a good way to interact with other companies and individuals. However, do this through a Facebook page, rather than a personal profile and don't 'friend' anyone on your personal profile who isn't a real friend.

- Instagram – particularly if you work in a creative industry consider joining Instagram and uploading pictures on a regular basis. Instagram is one of the fastest growing networks and with 300 million users (December, 2014) it has already overtaken Twitter. If you want visual exposure for your brand this is the place to be.

On all social networks check your privacy settings to make sure only those you want to see information about you can. Both LinkedIn and Facebook have rigorous privacy settings, but be aware that may not mean what you post can't be seen.

The golden rule is to think carefully about your digital brand, which mediums you are going to use and how, rather than use it haphazardly. Always have the mindset that every post is a layer added to your personal brand and potentially company brand too, so be strategic.

Effective networking

Let's get one thing clear to start with; networking is not about going to events to 'show your face' or to collect as many business cards as possible. Attending networking events is not really networking at all – it is merely part of the networking process for meeting new people and keeping in contact with others. It is more about setting the foundation for some good new relationships, and creating more visibility and exposure for your brand. In order to be effective at networking therefore, there needs to be a little more structure and planning than just turning up at events or attending them when you're free.

Some people will do anything to avoid going to networking events and others love it. Which camp do you fall into? Whatever the answer, networking in whatever form is a necessary activity in business today, but it need not be the chore that you might consider it to be.

Networking expert Andy Lopata (**www.andylopata.com**) sums this up by saying, 'Effective networking is far more reliant on the strong networks of people you surround yourself with. The reason why some senior executives find it easier to source support, ideas, introductions and referrals is that they have been able to build a bank of strong relationships over the years.' He adds: 'Many people say that it's not what you know, it's who you know' that's important today for helping to reach your career and visibility goals. In fact, it's even more than that – it's who knows you and what those people are saying about you behind your back, as we covered in Chapter 5. What are they saying right now to people they are with that you would love to meet?

So the real focus has to be on not just meeting people at a superficial level, it's about building those strong, trusted relationships. People you meet at networking events don't know you, therefore they are unlikely to give you the help or support you need from one short meeting. The trust and respect will take time to build.

Networking events are just one source of building a strong network. When it comes to attending these events there are some important factors to consider when you build these into your visibility plan:

- The right events – which ones are going to be the best ones for achieving the objectives you have? Given the work you have now done on your brand and what you want to be known for, actively look for events that are going to help raise your profile in line with your brand. Work with your communications department on this to highlight the best events for you to attend.

- What do you want to achieve? Having got a plan of the type of events you want to attend, with some scheduled in your calendar, now you need to work out what you want to achieve from each of them. It is knowledge of that sector, meeting specific people, assessing the event for a possible future speaking opportunity for you, establishing your personal presence within this environment, etc. Be clear about what you want to achieve and it'll make it easier to plan. For those of you not keen on attending these types of events, this will make it more project-based thereby creating a purpose.

- Do your preparation – Given that the purpose is to meet some key people and bearing in mind the points above, you need to create a plan to connect with around six people there who will be helpful to you in some way. Get the guest list in advance and plan this. Then ask yourself, what do you know about them already and what do you need to find out in advance?

Work on meeting people that you can build a good relationship with and not just 'make the sale' whatever the 'sale' might be. The business and personal rewards will be there if the relationship that is built is strong and trusted.

Andy Lopata's top tips for effective networking for you, and to adopt in your whole organization, include the following:

- Encourage a culture where networking is seen as a proactive, positive part of everyone's role, irrespective of his or her function. Create a connected company where staff are encouraged to develop strong networks, nurture those relationships and thus extend the reach of the organization.

- Don't judge success from networking events on the number of cards given or collected. Measure the number of follow-up meetings and, over the long term, the input of those new contacts into the organization in terms of business information, guidance, feedback and referrals.

- Encourage vulnerability and lead by showing it yourself. Don't expect any individual to have all of the answers, give permission for them to reach out to their network and ask. Build a diverse network around you, including people with a range of expertise and experience that adds to your own and those with a different way of looking at the world.

Your personal brand in the media

As we've now seen, in order for you to build real authentic personality into your company brand, as a senior leader you need to be out there and visible and this includes being in the media. You should no longer leave this activity to your chosen spokesperson only, but consider how and where are you best placed personally to be visible also.

Media appearances can be in many different forms, including your industry press (online and print), local radio and national and international television. Whatever form you decide on or end up contributing to, the biggest mistake you can make is not to be prepared or decide you can wing it. As well as preparing your content and key sound bites, you also need to ensure you have taken the necessary steps to be fully equipped with the know-how to handle whatever is thrown at you. Once it's said it's gone when it comes to media interviews. Nothing is off the record, even if you or the journalist says it is, and you will rarely have any control over an edit.

Treat every media interview as an opportunity to enhance your personal brand. Always consider what the key messages or points are that you must get across about your brand, as well as the subject matter of the interview. I'm not suggesting you hijack the interview with your own agenda, but don't lose sight of the principal reason why you're doing the interview. It's easy to forget in the heat of the moment in a live interview so you need to prepare. In addition, the interviewer does not really care about you and the benefit to you of being there; they are only interested in getting some interesting perspectives on the story in question.

Let me give you an example of what I mean. Several years ago I was asked to go on BBC News for a live TV interview about Cherie Blair (Tony Blair was then Prime Minister) spending a reported £7,700 on her hairdressing bill as she travelled with her husband on the election campaign. I did not want to be stereotyped as an image consultant commenting on image alone, but rather the deeper subject matter of personal branding and how this is portrayed. Therefore, my planned answer to the question that I knew was coming – 'Can this huge hairdressing bill be justified?' – was this: 'Cherie Blair has been criticized for her image numerous times over the years in her role as the Prime Minister's wife, and the media leap on every opportunity to do this. However, on this occasion, her appearance was not mentioned at all, positively or negatively during the campaign and it was only after the issue of the hairdressing bill emerged two weeks later that her appearance in any form was brought to the fore. Therefore, her appearance was considered appropriate throughout and it did not get in the way of the important elements of the campaign, that of the Prime Minster himself and his behaviours, actions and speeches. So yes, it was money well spent and can be justified.' My sound bite I chose to focus on was 'If your image is appropriate for the situation, then it doesn't get in the way of your true brand qualities and abilities'.

Always think about how you can weave in your agenda for the interview too. I interviewed the highly respected media coach Alan Stevens for his top tips for media interviews for executives. He said at the start: 'Great media communication is a real and necessary business asset, yet most executives fail badly at it.'

Here are Alan's top tips:

1 Know your core message

This is the most crucial aspect of media interaction. You must pre-plan your message, which should be brief, relevant and memorable. Use the core message or phrase at the start and end of your interview, if necessary by 'bridging' – for example: 'That's a good point, but the real issue here is...'

2 Tell your story

Use stories that have happened to you, not stories involving others. If you keep a lookout, there will be plenty of incidents you can use to make your point. It's easier to remember your stories, and they will not have been heard before. Never, ever use a story from someone else and pretend that it happened to you.

3 Be original

People are fascinated by originality. Your ideas are unique to you, and though they may have been influenced by others, will be yours alone.

4 Be controversial

Make yourself stand out by going against conventional wisdom, or delivering a rarely heard point of view. If you agree with everyone else, why communicate at all? There's no need to be critical of others, but giving solid reasons why you take another view is good content for interviews.

5 Provide evidence or proof

Always back up your ideas with evidence or proof via a real-life story, and make sure that you quote the source of the information so that it can be verified. If you can't find any evidence, you can either fall back on the old phrase 'in my long experience' or drop the idea.

6 Get out of the elevator

The elevator pitch, a short speech about what you do, used to be a fashionable way of opening a dialogue in an interview. However, talking at people for up to two minutes without a break is hardly a way to encourage them to warm to you. Instead, try offering a simple, intriguing response to start with.

7 Show you care

People love to see passion in communication. If you care about something, share your passion and people will respond. Even if they don't initially agree with you, they will appreciate your feelings about the subject, and may even be persuaded.

8 Drop the cliché

Using phrases like 'It's not rocket science' or 'Change is the only constant' won't have as much impact as normal speech. Alas, some people find it impossible to speak without using a cliché.

9 One message at a time

Media interviews are short, and can last less than one minute. Since your audience will recall only one thing, it makes sense to concentrate on your key message throughout, and repeat it at the end too.

10 Only say it if you really mean it

Authenticity is essential to good communication. If you lack conviction or, worse still, don't believe what you are saying, it will be obvious. Stick to content that you are confident about.

Having made many live broadcast media interviews myself, and written over 200 articles for publication in the global press, I've learned many things the hard way, and I would add some further tips to Alan's:

- Consider your outfit for TV interviews – simple and not too much pattern is best. Make sure there is nothing distracting that will get in the way of people listening 100 per cent to what you are saying. Check yourself in the monitor if at all possible before going live. There is nothing worse than a collar sticking up, a tie badly tied or a shirt gaping in the wrong place for distracting the viewer. The viewer will spend their time thinking subconsciously 'Why has somebody not fixed that?' or 'They don't appear very credible', rather than taking in the content of your interview.

- Wear make-up (yes, guys too) – high-definition TV has made it more necessary to have a professional apply make-up for you before a TV interview. Lights in a TV studio are harsh and make-up is needed even to maintain your normal appearance. You will notice a TV presenter's skin looks slightly orange, but on screen it looks normal. If you avoid the use of make-up you will look sallow and unhealthy in comparison. A shiny skin might not be noticeable until we see it close up, which is the case on screen. Make-up will help stop a shiny skin becoming a distraction to your words. Always take up the offer of make up at the studio before you go on air.

- Sound bites – be clear about the specific points you want to make and create simple sound bites for them. You can repeat these two or three times to ensure they get remembered, without overdoing it.

- Off-putting eye contact – something nobody tells you about live TV interviews is that the presenter will often break eye contact with you after asking the question, to look at their notes for the next question. This means you are left answering the question, looking at them but getting no eye contact back. You can often find yourself in a 'conversation' that is not engaging and that feels false. The presenter of course is only doing their job, but it can be very distracting for you, so it's good to be aware beforehand and perhaps practise the scenario with somebody. If you look uncomfortable, your brand and credibility will be affected.

- Even if you're promised a view of the article or interview before it goes to print, this rarely happens and you should not rely on it. Just focus on making sure you say only what you are happy with and nothing more.

Just some final tips to help preserve your reputation with the media:

- Provide useful content, not run-of-the-mill that everybody knows. Keep up to date on your topic area.

- Keep your content brief and to the point – don't waffle.

- Make sure you are easily contactable directly – sometimes interviews are required outside of normal office hours.

- Be responsive – return calls and e-mails from journalists promptly. They usually need interviews and content last minute and will go elsewhere if they can't get in touch with you.

- Never make false claims or say anything you can't substantiate.

- Don't tell a journalist or reporter how to do their job. Be polite and professional whatever they throw at you. As a very last resort, walk away if you need to.

On this last point, some media interviews could get tough especially if you're responding to something negative that has happened in your company or industry. While I would suggest you get specialist coaching in this area, one golden rule is never to lose your cool. The viewers or listeners will always hear the challenging questions, but how you respond is what they will remember most.

From reading this chapter, I trust you will be convinced that your visibility and exposure as a senior leader in your organization is not a choice any more. It is critical to your corporate brand reputation and adds the necessary layer of personality and 'realness' to how your company is perceived from the outside world as well as from your employees. Your personal brand is also enhanced by taking the brand you defined in Chapter 5 and further strengthening it with the strategic building of a visibility plan.

I strongly recommend that you don't leave your visibility to chance any longer, but rather take control of it and manage it in line with what the senior position you hold demands and requires.

References

Carson, E (2014) [accessed 12 October] 'Your Linkedin personal brand: 6 tips to build a strong one', TechRepublic, 13 May. Available from: www.techrepublic.com/article/your-linkedin-personal-brand-6-tips-to-build-a-strong-one/

Sampson, E (2002) *Build Your Personal Brand*, Kogan Page, London

Weber Shandwick (2015) [accessed 12 October] 'The CEO Reputation Premium: Gaining advantage in the engagement era', Weber Shandwick. Available from: http://webcache.googleusercontent.com/search?q=cache:u49l-e75VPcJ:www.webershandwick.com/uploads/news/files/ceo-reputation-premium-executive-summary.pdf+&cd=1&hl=en&ct=clnk&gl=uk

Presentational brand

07

A senior vice-president I once worked with said, 'One's ability to get promoted rests on one's ability to present well.' These are wise words indeed and could be applied to any enhancement you seek in exposure or in building your reputation.

We've covered in some detail how crucial the people element of your corporate brand is. There is simply nothing more powerful at projecting the personality of the brand than via your senior leadership team. The way your leaders present themselves publicly is a primary opportunity to cement all of your corporate brand messaging and bring it to life in the most compelling and convincing way possible.

There are many great books on effective presenting and you should certainly read some of them if you're serious about making a name for yourself as a great presenter, which you should be. We've seen in Chapter 6 how important it is to raise your visibility and exposure levels, and presenting well should be at the top of the list. People will talk about you and remember you for an engaging and memorable presentation. They will also go away with a refreshed view of your company brand and of you as an individual. It's your chance to get your 'story' across too.

Levels of trust can be elevated when you present on stage externally as a leader of your organization. What you say on a 'public' stage that is also quite possibly being recorded is considered to be accurate and believable, as why would you say it otherwise? Your words and portrayal of the company are therefore viewed as more trustworthy than any PR campaign can ever achieve.

Any presentation is about getting a message across clearly and can therefore apply equally to a formal stand up and present format, a team meeting update, a virtual presentation over video conference or a media interview. All of the content of this chapter will be relevant to each of these.

This chapter is not about traditional presentation skills. I'm assuming because of the level you operate at that you know the basics at least, and get to practise and present at regular intervals. My aim here is to provide you with the crucial factors to creating and presenting a memorable and authentic presentation that gets talked about, not just for content but for the impression of your personal brand and your corporate brand that you leave on your audience. I call this 'presentational brand' and in summary it's about the impression you leave an audience with of you and your company when you leave the stage. There is no better way to be seen and heard than presenting a relevant, meaningful and impactful message in a way that totally engages everybody in the audience to a level that they talk about you afterwards and do something with the message you presented. Your presentations will not just be internal, I'm sure; they will and should also be to external audiences if your aim is to raise your own and your company's profile and personality.

This content is based on my personal experience of presenting internationally for the past 15 years, also being in the audience of literally hundreds of talks around the world, together with my experiences of working with a large number of senior executives on their presentational brand via coaching. I have captured here for you the elements of presenting that I believe will make you stand out from the crowd authentically every time you present and help you to develop a strong brand both personally and for your company as a leading ambassador of your brand. I have focused only on the cream of presentational impact for this purpose, and those elements that should become a discipline for you when you prepare for the next opportunity to share a message.

An important concept to remember when preparing is that any presentation is designed to do one or more of the following:

- impart knowledge;
- persuade;
- motivate.

If you cannot confidently provide any of these outcomes then you have to question if your presentation is worthwhile or if indeed it might damage your brand or reputation.

In this chapter we'll be covering:

- the preparation process;
- the start and end;
- structuring for relevant content;
- making a key point stand out;
- storytelling and making it visual;
- pitching your presentation well;

- how you show up, non-verbally;
- Q & A;
- the tools for the job.

The 'P' word

You've heard it before, many times: 'Fail to prepare, prepare to fail'. It doesn't do any harm to hear this again. Very few people can pull off a good presentation with no preparation. When it comes to personal brand, it goes a little deeper than this – if you deliver a poor presentation with obvious lack of preparation, then not only does your presentation fail to hit the mark, but your brand suffers too. As we saw in Chapter 5 with the Pearl analogy, a significant diluting layer will have been added that may be difficult to recover from. It will have the effect, at best, of being unmemorable and your audience being indifferent to you and your content, to at worst a rippling effect of lack of respect due to poor preparation and loss of credibility due to flat delivery skills. Do you really want your brand to suffer in this way?

Of course, if you are part of the senior leadership team and this is a public presentation, or it's recorded for online viewing, then the impact could be worse. As we saw in Chapter 4, the brand of the leadership team is perceived by the outside world to be indicative of the brand of your organization. The corporate reputation can be heavily affected by one of your leaders delivering a poorly prepared presentation. It is easy to fall into the trap of thinking 'well this is content I know inside-out, there's no need to prepare and I'll just say what comes into my head at the time'. This is dangerous for several reasons – and it will be noticed and lose you credibility.

I'll always remember one particular time watching a consistently great presenter speak, Mark Sanborn from the United States. Mark is a friend of mine in the speaker world, and I've seen him present many times. He is highly experienced and very polished in his style and delivery. At one point in this particular presentation, Mark was listing three points he was going to cover. He listed two and forgot the third. He then nonchalantly reached into the inside pocket of his jacket, pulled out a card, reminded himself of the third point, put the card back in his pocket and carried on. You could feel the amazement in the room – not because he had forgotten the third point, but because somebody as experienced as Mark Sanborn had actually prepared notes in case of forgetting where he was. The respect levels for Mark increased even beyond where they were before.

Showing an audience that you have prepared with notes like this, that you have specific content in a particular order and that you don't want to miss out anything important, is always going to make a positive impression. If you are merely referring to them or glancing at them as a reminder when necessary, rather than reading a script or using them as a complete crutch, it shows respect for your audience and demonstrates that it's not just off the cuff. Too many people see using notes as a weakness – it's not, it's the sign of a true presenting professional.

The 'must haves'

A sure way to lose your audience is to have too much content for the time you have available to deliver it. You will always have important key points to get across and this is absolutely what you should stick to. No more, no less. If your presentation is more than 20 minutes long, then question it. Any audience is going to find it tough to concentrate and take in all you say if your presentation is longer. That's why TED talks (**www.TED.com**) are 18-minutes long – the optimum duration for any audience to absorb the content. In her research, learning specialist Abreena W Tompkins recommends using an interval of intense focus for 15 to 20 minutes followed by a break of two to three minutes. This could be a question asked of an audience, a brief group discussion or a fun interaction of some sort. Tompkins says online in Faculty Focus, 'Physiologically, your neurons are keen and alert for no more than twenty consecutive minutes. At the end of those twenty minutes, your neurons have gone from full-fledged alert to total collapse, and it takes two to three minutes for those neurons to be completely recovered and back to the total alert state' (Kelly, 2013).

Start with considering what it is your audience need to hear; what do you want them to go away with? Write these key points down. If somebody was unable to attend your presentation, how easy will it be for a person who was there to give the absent person the key points? Should they be able to clearly recall the message that you wanted to leave them with?

Now consider what information you absolutely need to support these key points. Your next task is to take out the nice-to-have or should-have items and just leave the must-have content to support your key points.

Just include the 'must-have' content

Start strong

Too many ineffective presentations start off with a run-of-the-mill 'Good morning, thank you for coming. I know the traffic today has been terrible so I appreciate you being here. Today I'm going to share with you...' In other words the dull unnecessary words that start a presenter off in second gear when really he or she should be in fifth gear right from the outset. An ongoing study into the concentration levels of an audience by communication expert Andy Bounds (**www.andybounds.com**) shows that an audience is at its most receptive and engaged right at the start of your presentation; their concentration dips in the middle, and picks up again towards the end. I've seen Andy carry out an exercise several times with audiences that demonstrates that this is true.

To test this out, Andy tells his audience he is going to put up 45 words, one by one, on slides. He tells them to take note of the words, not to write them down but to try to remember as many as they can as they are projected. He then tells them that in the middle somewhere, he's going to pause and say that these next few words to be projected are very important. He'll then go through to the end. When all words have been projected, he asks them all to write down as many words as possible that they remember. Then he puts up all the words on a slide together and asks them to check how many they have correct. The results are consistent every time he does this and he has tried it with over 200,000 people! Less than 1 per cent remember the last five words, but around 90 per cent remember the first five. This shows, of course, that people are heavily biased to the first things they hear and see. Around 15 per cent remember the words in the middle that were pointed out as important.

Why waste that all-important opportunity at the start to get your crucial content across? Don't wait until the middle or worse still the end, when the attention levels are low to share your best stuff. They might have switched off by the time you get to it. Changing the typical order of your presentation content works. Andy helped one bank win their largest-ever deal with this technique (over £2.6 billion), and another bank to win 18 sales pitches out of 18. This is quite a success rate.

> Put your best content at the start

Your start should relate to your overall key message. I coached a senior manager on his presentation to his board on absenteeism. During the coaching session he first started his presentation off slowly and with little impact or focus on the key message. We reworked it and here's how his start ended up: '11,000 hours – that's the total number of hours in absenteeism in this company, in a week across the country. It's enough to run another mega store for a month.' Then he went on to explain what he would be covering, the impact to the business and suggestions to rectify the situation.

Start with an impactful statement – it's refreshing and not many people do it well. Making the most of the first impression is essential to gain maximum engagement and impact. If you start weak, it's much harder to make up for it and recover.

A great structure

An audience will only follow you if you know where you are going! If an audience feels you have no structure or they don't know the direction you're heading, you will lose them very quickly. Think about the times when you've been in an audience and have no idea what the presenter is going to cover, where he or she is going to next and if you're going to hear what you want and need to hear. You're likely to switch off.

Having an odd number of points or areas you are going to cover is easier for an audience to follow than an even number. The power of three is also a good rule to follow. Let them know early on the number of points you are going to cover and what they are in overview. In her research, Abreena W Tompkins also covers this odd-number reasoning. She says the brain processes three or five items more efficiently than any even number. If you're going to present an audience with a list of six things you're going to cover and can't get them down to three or five, then present them in two groups of three. We can process things in groups and the brain responds to the 'whitespace' as Tompkins calls it, and we absorb points more effectively.

Make it visual

Engaging your audience should be at the forefront of your mind for your presentation, no matter how long or short, or how formal or informal. If you create a visual picture in the mind of your audience members, then they are more likely to remember what you've said and take it away to do something with. They can also recall it and share it more easily with others.

There are various ways to create visual images in people's minds:

- real-life examples and anecdotes;
- analogies;
- storytelling;
- simple images on slides;
- providing an emotion or feeling that in turn creates an image in the mind.

Often by using one or some of the above, it will allow another dimension of you and your brand to be exposed too, which increases the level of authenticity in your delivery and message. People will 'go with you' more if they feel you are being authentic and sincere and not trying too hard to perform.

To make a key point, a good structure to use is this:

- Make the point.
- Relate a story, anecdote, an analogy or give a visual example that supports the point and perhaps illustrates it in a diverse way.
- Make the application of the point back to the audience again. By this I mean make it relevant to them – what will this mean to them specifically in their life, role, environment.

Let me extend the earlier example for you:

- The point:

  11,000 hours – that's the total number of hours of absenteeism in the last week across the country.

- Relate a story or a visual proof:

  Put another way, that's enough to run another mega store for a whole month. These are photos we took of the Southern Head Office last month – you can clearly see the number of empty desks.

- Make the application:

  11,000 absenteeism hours equates to $1.3 million of lost man-hours every month, and almost $8 million in a six-month period. As a consequence, the manpower return on investment is almost 20 per cent lower than the same period last year. Clearly a solution is required urgently.

Relevance

This structure gives your audience an opportunity to totally absorb your point in three different ways, giving you the best possible chance to ensure its impact and stickiness.

Making the point relevant to the audience is crucial – it needs to make sense to them in their world in order to have the desired impact. For example, you could be delivering the same presentation to different departments within your company but you must ensure that the message lands as you need it to for each audience member. If your message is about the need for 'living the brand' throughout the organization, then for your senior level of management the relevancy for them might be more about the results of 'living the brand' increasing share price or market share, by having the employee base represent the brand. For other levels of the employee base, it might be more about career progression and getting noticed if they truly live and represent the brand. Unless a message resonates with the individual you're unlikely to get resulting action. By including some elements of personality, with examples and anecdotes, you will bring a level of reality and authenticity to your delivery that in addition gives out a piece more of you as an individual and adds another dimension to your brand.

When you are considering the relevancy to your audience, you also need to think about where they are at right now with regard to your message or topic. Do they care? Is this a sensitive subject? Are they anxious about their job? If you need to present a negative message that is likely to further compound anxiety about job losses for example, then you will need to address this concern upfront and show that you understand their anxieties. Then find the positive slant on this, perhaps that with change comes opportunity for everybody to seek out.

The message will land more effectively with them if they feel you are talking directly to them individually, and will help to build a connection between you and them. For example, you could also refer to a situation demonstrating that you are aware of a recent particular challenge or better still perhaps a successful outcome with a project, and use some of the specifics to support a point you are making.

In summary, preparing your presentation with the audience in mind is critical to the success of landing your message in the intended way. It also speaks volumes about you as a brand and your reputation is enhanced.

Storytelling

Adopt the rule-of-thumb that all your presentations should include some sort of story, anecdote or real-life experience. Without this, you are almost guaranteed to fail to engage your audience as effectively as you want and need to.

We discussed the espresso effect in Chapter 5, to help you to recall pivotal moments in your life that can lead to developing your own personal stories. These stories can then provide a basis for illustrating and reinforcing your business messages in a way that is compelling and memorable to an audience.

To help you pull out these relevant stories consider the following example starting lines:

- Let me tell you about a time...

- Imagine yourself...

- Let me take you back to...

- Picture this...

- Four years ago...

- When I was six years old, my grandmother once said...

- There was a time when...

- When I first started...

- As an example...

- What if...

- Was there a time when...

- My teacher once said to me...

- In 10 years' time, it will look like this...

I'm sure you'll think of others, and ideas will flow when you focus some time on getting your example stories together. I always find it useful to record in my iPhone, humorous situations, stressful times when travelling, and general observational anecdotes that might be useful for creating stories. I would encourage you to do the same and make it a habit whenever you're out and about and in particular in other countries or unusual places. Once your brain is focused on this, you'll be amazed at how you spot the opportunities.

You might well now be thinking that you don't know where to start with constructing your stories for your presentations. Here are some tips that will help, provided by storytelling genius Doug Stevenson – **www.storytelling-in-business.com**. Remember your stories can be anything from two to five minutes ideally. Make sure they are relevant and that the length is appropriate for the total duration of your presentation and the point you are making. If they are longer than five minutes, then you must have a very powerful point to make with the story.

Nine steps for story structure

1 **Set the scene**. Create the context within which the story takes place. What do we need to know about the time, place, atmosphere and circumstances for the story to make full sense? Think about using any and all of the five senses.

2 **Introduce the characters.** Whenever there are other people in the story – the main characters other than you – describe them so that the audience can see them and relate to them. Include anything pertinent about your relationship with them and describe a unique quirk that brings them to life. Introduce characters where they occur naturally in the narrative, not necessarily in the second step of the nine steps.

3 **Begin the journey.** What is the journey from safety to danger or from the known into the unknown? In other words, what is the goal or the task to be accomplished? It doesn't have to be profound.

4 **Encounter the obstacle.** Something or someone gets in your way or impedes your progress. What is it? What went wrong? Make sure the obstacle is clearly defined so that the audience gets it. If you don't have an obstacle, you don't have a very powerful story; you may just have a vignette, which may be fine too. If you are developing a signature story, you will definitely need an obstacle.

5 **Overcome the obstacle.** This is where the teaching and relevancy occurs in your story. How did you overcome the obstacle? Analyse your thought process. What did you do?

6 **Resolve the story.** Let us know how things worked out in the end and clean up any loose ends.

These next two points relate back to my earlier point about making it relevant and meaningful to the audience.

7 **Make the point.** What is the point or the lesson learned? Be concise – there should be only one point for each story. Try to make your point using a succinct phrase that will be remembered.

8 **Ask the question.** Ask a rhetorical question that transfers the point from your story to the audience, making them think.

9 **Repeat the point.** Repeat the point – use the same language as in number 7 or use your memorable phrase.

If you'd like to take your storytelling to another level, I can highly recommend Doug Stevenson's Story Theatre. Storytelling is an art but is simple to learn, and I would add, is an essential tool in effective business communication today. It will take your presentational brand to a level you've quite possibly not reached before and it's fun to do.

Getting the level right

There is often a fundamental incongruence between the way we present a message and the way in which the audience receives it. If we are to get our message across in the way we intend, we simply have to pay attention to this possibility to avoid it happening.

Very often a presenter will tend to pitch the presentation at an inappropriate level, particularly at the start. It is worth bearing in mind that your audience will quite possibly be at a different level to you when they start to receive your message. You only have a short space of time in which to win over the audience in order for them to decide you are worth listening to.

If you're pitching an idea or a project or something for which you need absolute buy-in, you need to hit the ground running and maximize that first impression. Oren Klaff, in his book *Pitch Anything* and in his interview on YouTube with London Live, talks about three levels of the brain – the neocortex (complex brain – the smart, problem-solving and mathematical), the mid-brain (processes social situations) and the crocodile brain (thinks very simply) (Klaff 2011).

Although Klaff writes about pitching in a highly pressurized environment mainly in the investment banking world, we can learn much from his 'one bite of the apple' approach to getting instant buy-in, and use it to create a powerful presentational brand that we become known for. Presenters often want to include complex information as they believe their audience needs to hear this, or to try to establish a level of credibility. However, audiences are pretty much always at the crocodile or simplest brain level when they first receive information. When we are confronted with a situation, our immediate thoughts are around 'fight or flight', should I stay and listen or should I switch off and leave. The crocodile brain wants things quickly, summarized, visual and black and white. Then it filters out what's important. We talked about first impressions in Chapter 1 and taking in the non-verbal communication first – this is all part of crocodile brain process. It's instant, clear and forms the basis of what we do next. At the start of a presentation, we tend to give the audience the detail of the challenge or message, or of what we are trying to 'sell', but they are more likely to be thinking to themselves 'is this useful information, is it going to be easy to understand, do I need to hear it, is it useful to me or even does this person come across as credible, professional, authentic etc?' They are at the simplest level right at the start and often we will over-complicate the content and not address the very questions in their minds at this point.

Using humour

Getting some fun into your content is an important element to include. It provides people with a chance to 'download' the serious points to their mind, and adds another positive layer to your personal brand. However, it is also a danger area for your brand. Telling jokes is rarely a positive component in a presentation, unless after dinner, but if delivered well, including humorous stories or experiences can be a compelling way to engage an audience. Always practise your humour on others and tweak the wording or timing where necessary. Minor aspects and adjustments can make a massive difference to whether the story gets the desired effect or not. If your humour can relate to an experience or an observation that everybody can identify with, then it is more likely to generate the reaction you need.

A few years ago I was presenting to an audience of 350 professional speakers in December in Nova Scotia at 9 am. The night before at 2 am a fire alarm sounded and the message that continually came over the public address system was 'The fire alarm systems have been activated – there is no cause for concern at this time. Please do not use the elevators.' Now wide awake, I heard this message over and over again thinking that they've said 'No cause for concern', so I need to stay put. However, about 20 minutes into this repetitive announcement I suddenly thought perhaps I should be leaving the room and go outside. The message was not clear. At that point, my first consideration was not the −11° temperature outside, nor the fact that there may actually be a fire, but instead that in about seven hours' time I would be presenting to an audience of 350 professional speakers, on brand and image, with a personal brand and image to keep up myself, with bed-hair and no make-up! How crazy was I?

I decided then to work on building this experience into my presentation for the next morning. The story caused considerable laughter and, of course, empathy from the women especially and it took a while for the audience to calm down again.

I told the same story a few weeks later at another conference presentation for a group of lawyers – I got totally the opposite response. There was no reaction whatsoever and the humour went flat. This was, of course, partly to do with the fact they hadn't experienced the fire alarm situation with me as the previous audience had, but mainly that the wording and delivery needed work to be effective for another audience. I have since worked on this story with a coach and it now creates the desired impact again, albeit not to the same level as the first time.

Rehearse your humour

Working with a humorist to get the desired level of fun into your presentation is highly recommended. I work with the great speaker and humorist Tim Gard from Colorado in the United States. This is a truly worthwhile investment of time. Watching true masters of humour in action too is an excellent action point for developing great presentational brand and style. Look up Jeanne Robertson (**www.jeannerobertson.com**) – a true connoisseur of observational humour in her presentations, and George Campbell speaker and comedian, who presents under the make-believe name of Joe Malarkey (**www.joemalarkey.com**).

In short, pretty much every presentation should have an appropriate level of humour added, that reinforces a point you are making. If it's irrelevant it may backfire and confuse your message.

Looking the part

Too often most focus is put on the content and structure of a presentation and very little in comparison with the delivery mechanisms and the non-verbal elements. However, if the non-verbal communication of your message is not in alignment with your message or gets in the way somehow, your hard-worked content will never land as you need it to. If you're on stage, things like dress and appearance are often scrutinized more, albeit sub-consciously by most of the audience; and of course they are magnified if you're projected on a large screen. When you're preparing your presentation, consider what is the most appropriate outfit. Ask yourself:

- Who are the audience and what are they expecting?
- What is the situation or environment?
- What are your personal objectives?

If you consider these questions you will come up with the right outfit. With a smart-casual dress code often in place in organizations today, this can create an added level of complexity to the question of what is appropriate. General guidelines for smart-casual are to apply similar rules to your formal look – good fit, current, sharp not sloppy and appropriate level of casual. Not building this into your planning could significantly dilute the impact you will make. The non-verbal impression is the very first piece of information people absorb about you.

In addition to this, I will mention here other considerations for you regarding dress and appearance that I've found let presenters down most of all and get in the way of the message. This is by no means an exhaustive list of items, however it provides some food for thought on the major areas to think about. You can refer to my book *Drop Dead Brilliant* for more information on dress and appearance.

- **Good fit**. Many a time I have watched a presenter deliver a great presentation, only to be irritated by the distraction of ill-fitting clothes. Hard-earned professional credibility can be severely diluted by ignoring this. Poor fit is such a simple point to fix if, first, time is taken to think about it consciously and then to get advice on what needs altering. Common areas of bad fit are sleeves and trousers too long or short, shirts too tight and jackets too big or tight when the buttons are done up. These are all areas that can easily be fixed by a local tailor or somebody who specializes in alterations. Most good clothing retailers today will provide an alteration service, as do dry-cleaners.

  As a guide, jacket sleeve length should finish just where the thumb joint meets the wrist. Too long, and it looks like you've borrowed the jacket; too short and it looks like an old one you've grown out of. Either way, whatever you spend on your jackets and suits, they will look cheap if they don't fit well.

  Trousers for men should fold just once onto the shoes, not three or four times so there are multiple folds. For women, they should be one or two inches above the ground, covering the foot.

  If you are going to button your jacket for a more formal look, make sure it doesn't stretch across your front. It is best practice for men to leave the bottom button undone.

- **Shoes**. When you're presenting these get noticed – especially if you're on a raised platform or stage. Never assume people won't notice them, or worse still avoid even considering them. It seems basic common sense; however, in my experience it's not common practice to ensure your shoes are polished, not scuffed and appropriate for the level you work at. Again it's an area where I would suggest you get some feedback.

- **Well-maintained.** Please do pay attention to loose hems and buttons, and any marks or stains. Don't fall into the trap of thinking nobody will notice – they always do! Shiny trouser seats or jackets, due to over-wearing, are a complete no-no, as is see-through fabric in dresses and skirts. Check it out with light behind you, including the lit screen for your slides.

Finally, always do a full-length check in the mirror before you stand up and present. It's well worth the effort in checking if anything is out of place or needs attention. Golden rule, get a third party to provide feedback for an important presentation especially – often others can provide insight that you can miss or haven't thought of yourself.

As a senior leader it is also worth considering your own individual style and brand image with your wardrobe. Fashion historian James Laver once said, 'Clothes are inevitable. They are nothing less than the furniture of the mind made visible.' It's also worth an amusing look at his Laver's Law – his view of the complex cycle of fashion change. It says: 'Ten years before its time, a fashion is indecent; ten years after, it is hideous – current is smart.' Take a look at your wardrobe and make sure your outfits are up to date and not more suitable to your brand five or more years ago.

We do feel we get something about the personality of the individual from the way they choose to dress. Your unique style is not something that is easy to decide on yourself if you want to tweak it, so get specialist advice. Your wardrobe is all part of your brand and should be right up there with other elements of how you project yourself.

Body indicators

I consider the term body language overused and people can get too hung up on it. Finding your own natural style when you present is the most import-ant part. If you're fairly understated in your style that's fine, and if you're more expressive naturally that's fine too. Just don't try to be somebody you're not. Having said that, there are some gestures that can get in the way of your message, the same way as other non-verbal elements can. Over-exuberant arm gestures, for example, will distract unless that is your natural extrovert style. The best way to address this is to get feedback from a selection of people from different presentations you deliver in different environments. A word of warning – watching yourself on video can give you a false perspective. What is seen on a screen can exaggerate what an audience actually sees so best to get live observation feedback.

In terms of non-verbal communication while presenting, the brilliant human behavioural expert John Demartini seems to break all the rules, yet still manages to captivate an audience every time with his totally unique and natural style with lack of eye contact, expressive gestures and pacing around the stage. The reason being it looks right for him, so the audience is comfortable that he is comfortable and therefore they focus on his content more.

Being heard

We are not the best judge of our own voice – in fact we often dislike it because when we hear it on a recording it sounds totally different to how we hear it ourselves when speaking. Or perhaps somebody told you once that your voice was too high-pitched and it's stuck with you. Therefore, the best starting point to ensuring your voice has the level of impact it needs, is to ask a few colleagues to give you specific feedback on clarity of voice, intonation (the rise and fall of the voice), modulation (variation), pitch (high or low) and pace. Use the feedback chart at the end of this chapter to get feedback on voice and other elements of your presentation.

Do remember that without a good delivery system in your voice, your message will not have the desired impact. We can all recall a great teacher or college lecturer who knew his or her content, but just could not hold our interest as their voice was dull, monotone or not easily understood. Don't waste your next opportunity to deliver with great content, and simply ignore the need to ensure your voice can convey accordingly.

Think about how a good lawyer sums up his defence in a court of law to a jury after a long trial. He will deliver with moderate and deliberate pace, never rush, emphasize key words, pause between key points, and modulate the voice well in order to keep attention, engage and make it easy to listen. You can also consider how you might read a book to a four-year-old child. You work hard to keep their attention as they switch off easily without the modulation in the voice, changes in tone and volume, and general variation. It's worth being aware of the fact that adult audiences are no different to children; in fact we're probably worse as we have so much going on in our heads at any one time. We can easily 'leave the room' in our minds and lose attention if the voice of the presenter is weak or dull. I would advise you to consider rehearsing your presentation with one or both of these scenarios in mind – you'll never exaggerate, but it could help to improve the impact in your voice.

Be yourself

I believe one of the most important delivery elements of your presentational brand is being yourself. If you over-perform you will lose your authenticity and sincerity and possibly trust too. However, being you is not easy. When presenting, it is natural to fall into some form of performance style. Try to be as conversational as is appropriate for the setting and audience – build in personal stories and experiences to aid this, refer to real situations and use people's names etc. One of the biggest compliments I can personally get is that I am the same on-stage as I am off-stage and that people feel they know me just from listening to me speak. I refer you back to Chapter 5 where you thought about your personal brand and what you want to be known for – bring some of this brand out in every presentation and add layers with your unique stories that expose another dimension of you.

Sharp finish

Your ending is as important as your start – a lacklustre ending will seriously detract from your ability to influence your audience. It's your last chance to drive home your key messages and be remembered for the right reasons. There can be a tendency to appear to run out of gas at the end and come to an abrupt stop. For example, 'Well, that's about it' or 'OK, we're done.' You can summarize your points but bear in mind your audience may switch off if they feel you are repeating yourself. You need to have more than just a summary – a statement similar to how you approached the start is needed. You need to make it relevant and intellectual, and it could be humorous, unexpected or entertaining also – something that will be remembered and talked about. Here are a few suggestions for you, although of course there are many more options:

- A well-known or famous quote but followed by your own take
  on it – for example: 'Anna Morrow Lindberg once said, "The most

exhausting thing to be is inauthentic."' Followed by: 'Be yourself – be your own brand and build your reputation in alignment with your personal values. With authenticity comes consistency of brand.'

- A sound bite – and remember the power of three, from earlier in this chapter. Think Nike – 'Just Do It' – or your own: 'So if we're going to change the status quo with this challenge today, we need to think clarity, innovation and agility, or CIA.'

- A provocative statement or question – 'What you think your brand is, is quite probably not so in the eyes of others. Today is the day to start taking control of those perceptions.'

Having a great ending will allow people to sum up your message in their own heads too. It's your duty to make it easy for them.

Q & A

How many times have you witnessed an average presenter and then found that they absolutely come to life authentically during the Q & A or panel discussion later? I've seen this many times and found myself feeling frustrated that they hadn't been more themselves during the presentation. I would suggest you always look for an opportunity to have this type of informal discussion afterwards. Knowing you have this in place, also allows you more freedom to leave out presentation content that is not a must-have. I understand it may not always be possible to have a Q & A, and that you may sometimes have to conform to a structure. However, it's a good idea to consider this as part of your preparation and see if it's a possibility. A word of warning though: never finish your presentation on Q & A – always bring it back to you to end with your killer ending, rather than on what could be a negative question.

The most persuasive element

In relation to making an impact and your brand being portrayed positively – think about use of any slides as the final piece of your preparation, not the start. Have the mindset of 'do they add anything to my message' and if they don't, then leave them out. The most persuasive element of your presentation is you, not what's on your slides. If they serve no purpose they will serve to distract the focus from you, diluting your impact. Having said that at times of course they can add a powerful reinforcement of the point you are making. Images on slides tend to have a better impact in this respect, so seek to find a way to add to your message pictorially with slides, rather than text that you can say much more intensely yourself.

The right tools for the job

Audiovisual tools can be a fabulous aid of course to enhancing your presentation delivery, and are often critical to the success. However, they can also create an added potential hazard. Preparing for this will help to avoid or perhaps lessen the blow of what inevitably will happen at some stage in your professional career. Again with the focus on your present-ational brand, I'm going to provide you here with the pertinent points to look out for, all coming from my experience as a professional speaker with a personal brand to protect.

Microphones

My rule of thumb is if the audience size is over 50 then a microphone is needed. Although your voice might be strong, it can struggle if you have 50 people in a room. Even though they're listening most of the time, they may be engaged in group discussions and interaction, and being heard will present a challenge. You can also damage your voice if you have to keep the volume levels up over a period of time.

Unless you are personally comfortable and know how to use a hand-held microphone effectively, always request a lapel microphone. This way you can move around more freely and use your arms better if this is your style. Make sure you request one in advance as not all venues provide them automatically. This is of course especially important if you're speaking at an external event. For ladies, an added piece of advice is to make sure you request one with a clip on the power pack, unless you have suitable pockets in a jacket. You can always purchase your own of course if you speak regu-larly to large audiences. Tuck the cables away so they are invisible and not a distraction.

Unless there is a good reason to stand behind a lectern to speak from the microphone there, then avoid it. You create a barrier between you and the audience, which is never conducive to creating rapport.

Remote presenter

Buy yourself a wireless remote presenter for your PowerPoint slides. It is much more professional than constantly leaning over the laptop to change slides, and gives you far more control over them rather than them controlling you. You can be at any place in your moving space to change slides and your presentation will flow more easily for you and your audience.

Be sure to blank out your slides with the B key when you have finished referring to them to bring the attention back to you – your remote presenter should have a function to do this.

Presentational brand feedback checklist

Getting regular feedback on your presentational brand is the only way you can truly improve your skills and have the confidence to know that you are making the desired impact. Try using this feedback chart and ask trusted colleagues and your teams to complete for you.

> 1 = not at all   5 = very

Opening

1 High impact	☐	**3** Relevant	☐
2 Got my interest	☐	**4** Memorable	☐

Voice

1 Easy to listen to ☐

2 Well-paced ☐

3 Good intonation (the rise and fall of the voice) ☐

4 Good variation ☐

5 Good pitch (highness and lowness) ☐

6 Good use of pauses ☐

Body indicators (language)

1 Distracting ☐

2 Effective ☐

3 Appears relaxed and comfortable ☐

4 Natural ☐

Content

1 Good use of stories and examples ☐

2 Clear messages ☐

3 Relevant to the audience ☐

4 Good use of humour ☐

5 Engaging ☐

6 Inspired to take action ☐

Visual aids (slides)

1 Relevant ☐

2 Clear ☐

3 Supportive to the messages ☐

Ending

1 Memorable ☐

2 Effective ☐

3 Finished on time ☐

4 Called for action ☐

Summary

My intention in this chapter has been to focus on the most pertinent elements for enhancing your presentational brand, and for increasing the personality of your corporate brand via you as a senior leader in your organization. My guess is you will be reasonably proficient at presenting already and quite possibly therefore may have fallen into some bad habits or to have become complacent when it comes to your preparation. I would suggest you use this chapter as a checklist each time you present and particularly focus on building your unique presentational brand. As a leader, becoming a great presenter is worth more to your corporate brand personality than you've probably even considered before. Although we can all think that our clients decide to buy our brand because of functional benefits of the product or service, it all comes down to how they 'feel' when they buy or associate with our brand. You and your leadership team can go a long way to ensuring this emotional connection with your brand is a consistently positive one, by personally connecting with audiences, whoever and wherever they are.

References

Kelly, R (2013) [accessed 12 October 2015] Brain-Based Online Learning Design, Faculty Focus, 24 January. Available from: www.facultyfocus.com/articles/online-education/brain-based-online-learning-design/

Klaff, O (2011) *Pitch Anything: An innovative method for presenting, persuading, and winning the deal*, McGraw-Hill, New York

Final words

08

This book has taken you on a journey exploring how you can add a dimension of personality to your corporate brand that you may not have considered or implemented before. We are entering a new business era where the human element and authenticity that people bring to your brand is your greatest opportunity for differentiation. Furthermore, it is an area that can no longer be overlooked, pushed aside or halfheartedly addressed. The personality of your brand cannot be copied by your competitors – it is your unique brand fingerprint and creates a brand message that represents who you are and what you stand for more powerfully than your PR and advertising campaigns can ever do.

The level of positive and consistent customer experience that you can create if your employees and leaders are fully engaged with your brand messaging and are able to internalize the values in their own authentic way, is your gateway to creating a true 'personality of the brand' identity.

The employer brand that is so important today as a magnet to your business is not just about great advertising campaigns or traditional talent sourcing methods it is interwoven with the way your employees behave to such a degree that the two are impossible to separate. Ask yourself: would you be happy for your employees to put all they know about your working culture into a book? Do you really know what they think about working for you and how your company makes them feel and, consequently, how they project your brand with their everyday behaviours and interactions? Are you measuring this employee engagement correctly and getting accurate feedback? What are you doing with that feedback that is necessary for really bringing about change?

We have four generations in our workplace today who are very different in the way they view life and work. Therefore you cannot continue to operate in the way you have always done and expect your organization's brand to be sustained. The true authenticity of the corporate brand needs to be visible and proven. What better way to do this than via your most valuable assets – your employees and your senior leadership team?

Your leaders are crucial to the personality of the brand experience that your stakeholders should have and deserve. They serve to create the workplace culture needed for optimum employee brand and for illustrating the highest quality of employer brand via their ability to brand themselves. Together with strong leadership visibility (internally, digitally, publicly on a stage and via the media) it provides the most compelling and differentiating opportunity for your company to be seen as relevant and appealing to your target audiences. This in turn will attract and retain the desired talent of tomorrow, and create trust, respect and authenticity for your customers to enjoy.

My hope is that you will take the messages of this book and use them to start bringing together a brand strategy that encompasses people behaviours, with as much focus as the traditional elements of branding into which you plough significant investment. Wouldn't it be great for positive experiences to increase and to become an accepted norm with outcomes of consistent customer experience, and for a lack of trust and respect to become a thing of the past and be the exception to the rule?

INDEX